The Authority Code

Use The Exact Formula to Become
The Hunted vs. The Hunter
For More Leads, Sales and Profits

by

T. Allen Hanes

Published by T. Allen Hanes Publishing Group, Houston, TX.

The Publisher has strived to be as accurate and complete as possible in the creation of this book.

This book is not intended for use as a source of legal, business, accounting or financial advice. All readers are advised to seek services of competent professionals in legal, business, accounting, and financial fields.

In practical advice books, like anything else in life, there are no guarantees of income made. Readers are cautioned to rely on their own judgment about their individual circumstances and to act accordingly.

While all attempts have been made to verify information provided in this publication, the Publisher assumes no responsibility for errors, omissions, or contrary interpretation of the subject matter herein. Any perceived slights of specific persons, peoples, or organizations are unintentional.

Manufactured & Printed in the United States of America.

Cover Design: T. Allen Hanes

ISBN: 978-1537294650

Publisher: T. Allen Hanes Publishing Group

Dedication

∞

Dedicated
to
Those Who Dream & Make Great Things Happen—
For Themselves and For the World.

It All Starts With You
Awakening Boldly To Yourself
As A True Authority.

∞

FOREWORD

Chances are that you can relate to this scenario: You are craving clients. You get anxious to hunt a sale—any sale...at any cost. Desperation has made you forget that "*You are the hunted*...not the hunter." The great news is that you can now shift the scenario.

With T. Allen Hanes' new breakthrough book *The Authority Code*, he reminds us—ever so cleverly—that to win in the game of business, never let prospective clients see you sweat, look inept, appear desperate, or seem needy. You are the expert with the subject matter or service industry expertise they are seeking...

To boldly and confidently convey your expertise, crack The Authority Code. Because of this book, that's not hard to do. In this semi-narrative, Hanes hand delivers all the necessary clues to debunk myths about claiming your authority and landing successful sales.

The Authority Code gives entrepreneurs valuable insight on how to market their expertise from a place of strength, not weakness. It reveals ways to shift your mindset and embrace the power of your authority, which unleashes your influence in the marketplace.

In weaving his own personal journey throughout the pages of this book, Hanes richly shares the real-life strategies he employed to become the well-established expert within his field.

Read this thoughtful work diligently. Apply the code dutifully. It is sure to help you release the full power of your authority. Then, go on to clinch more clients, make more sales, and increase profits as you simultaneously improve more lives.

Sharon Frame
Leadership Authority/Former
CNN Anchor
www.sharonframespeaks.com

Table of Contents

Introduction

If success results from a series of actions, what direction do you think the journey to success takes you on? Many people think it is a diagram with a straight line that starts from at the bottom and then ends at the top. Perhaps you have seen that unrealistic diagram changed with a zig-zag diagram instead that goes up, down, left, right as it zig-zags around again and again—until you end up in the upward position of success. Becoming an authority in your market has the potential to reduce your zig-zag directions and take it to an upwards position. *The Authority Code* is focused on showing you how you can quickly and easily use some of the well-kept secrets to position yourself as the top authority in your market and leverage it to get leads, sales and profits.

I have been in the zig-zag state for over 50 years—and just now in recent years have a path that is going upward. Yes, I have had successes along the way in various ways, but there have been many learning curves and failures along the way that are now contributing to my upward momentum of successes.

If you know that this zig-zag diagram is what is "the norm for success" for the stages involved in both developing your expertise as well as marketing your expertise, you can prepare yourself and your mindset to handle that so that you just take action on faith and remain calm in the process because it will all work out. However, you may need to do some resets, adjustments, and shifts along the way to change direction. The good news is that with the right mindset, it is all experience that is part of the process as you move towards success.

Before you even achieve success in reality, you need to achieve success in your mind with the right mindset. Being able to have the "authority stature" is partly achieved in being great at what you do as well as in having a significant presence in your market.

As Sun Tzu said in *The Art of War*, "When you are small, you need to appear big." Business is not war, but the competition can be steep. So, the same principle of "appearing big" applies to you when you want to be seen as an authority. This important point goes for entrepreneurs, local small business owners, consultants, service professionals, authors, speakers and coaches because they can use these techniques to position themselves to be the go-to person in their market.

In this book, I share how you can use The Authority Code Formula to do just that—position yourself as the authority in your industry. I will also show you how you can be featured on affiliate sites, such as ABC, NBC, CBS and Fox.

When you consider all of this information that you can apply, it is very important to "remember the chicken and the egg" to help identify prioritized actions. Does the chicken come first? Or is it the egg?

How this analogy relates to establishing perceived authority and celebrity status is connected to the following two questions:

> 1) Do you want to wait and hope that The Media might talk about you someday because you spent hours calling yourself the expert?
>
> 2) Or would you rather have others see you as the expert right now because The Media is talking about you today?

Yes, the choice in how you view it is up to you and what actions you take to position yourself.

Celebrity and authority status rarely just happen.

Take into account The Kardashian Effect. They are always deliberately creating and reinforcing a purposeful plan of action to manufacture their celebrity. The good news is that you can, too, find ways to be newsworthy—except around your branding and expertise. So, that is how you can "appear big" even if you are not...yet.

By sharing the secrets hidden within *The Authority Code*, you are no longer at an unfair advantage. It has rarely been talked about outside of insider circles.

The reason I wrote *The Authority Code*: *Use The Exact Formula to Become The Hunted vs. The Hunter For More Leads, Sales and Profits* is to help you position yourself within your market as the dominant, go-to authority expert so that you claim the success you deserve. I have personally experienced the journey from being the hunter to now becoming the hunted, which has provided the increased leads, sales and profits using this exact code that I have unlocked for myself and others who want the same thing.

The title *The Authority Code* refers to the code or combination of factors that culminate in achieving authority status. With a code, not only must a certain combination come together, but it must come together in the right formulaic order in order to unlock what was previously unavailable until the code was broken.

It is at that point when you gain access to what was unavailable as well as the benefits of it. In this case, positioning yourself and connecting your name with your authority positioning as a particular expert in your field is essential and helps you unlock increased leads, sales and profits as well as make more difference in the world.

As you go along, you are not only living your passion and building your dream, you are also building your legacy. The authority-building process needs to first be launched to lay a foundation to build upon, yet similar actions are repeated with variation to reinforce, maintain, and expand your authority.

Because it is a cyclical process that compounds, even throughout the book you will find repetition of important aspects of building your authority. It is actually a benefit that even though there are separate, yet inter-related code components for you to complete that they provide you with progress while simultaneously reinforcing other actions you have and/or will be taking again and again.

Because I am continually innovating and creating new content and approaches related to positioning myself and my clients as authorities, it is worth noting that elsewhere within my products and services that there is similar content where I have packaged authority-building elements are ones I have referred to as "The Authority Platform" and "The Authority Wheel."

By viewing it as a code to be followed, it streamlines the process even more so you can see that with each component that you are building layer upon layer of authority that gives you an even stronger foundation of staying relevant.

As an authority, you are the "author" or the "originator" or the "source" who brings the expertise to your market.

Even if there are other experts in your market, the assumption behind this book is that you have already developed your expertise within your market to the extent that you are a top expert before you claim your authority.

If you have not done so yet, it is important to do what it takes to build that expertise first. However, many times people are ready for months—if not years—before they ever do step out there as the authority that they already are.

The benefit of positioning yourself as the go-to expert is that it is "emotional shorthand" because once you position yourself as such, people will not only seek you in your market, but will be more willing to pay more to do business with you than they will with your competitors.

There are some common myths about authority that are not set in stone and are good to be aware of as they may help you move forward sooner than you might otherwise.

- Myth #1 – An expert is someone who calls themselves the expert, which makes them an expert.
- Myth #2 - An expert knows everything about their subject matter.
- Myth #3 - An expert is the very best at what they do in their field.

- Myth #4 – An expert has to work for years to build an expert reputation so that big online media outlets will talk about them as an authority.

If you find yourself buying into any of these myths and allowing yourself to be held back by them, it is important for you to recognize them individually and/or collectively so you can see them for what they are and move beyond them.

Yes, you do need to be great at what you do to the extent that you recognize that you can be confident in what you do know and can approach any areas that you do not know yet with confidence to figure out what you need to do if something new comes up for you.

Positioning yourself as an educator and an advocate as the go-to authority is for entrepreneurs, for local small business owners, for consultants, for service professionals, for authors, for speakers, for coaches, and so forth who can use these techniques to position themselves to be the expert in their market.

Whether you are a potential entrepreneur, a new entrepreneur, or a seasoned entrepreneur, leveraging your authority in a powerful way is vital to increasing your success.

There has never been a better time in the history of mankind than right now to be an entrepreneur because you have the opportunity to broadcast to the world using technology.

After I broke through barriers, embraced the broad opportunity available to entrepreneurs now, and began achieving ever-increasing levels of success, I started to write as well as to encourage and mentor others.

This book provides you with a key resource that can guide you along towards achieving success as an entrepreneur, whether you are just starting out or are already further down the pathway.

What you will most likely find out is that sometimes there is an opportunity for a while in your market, but then it changes. You have to be open to change. You may realize the need to change direction because you recognized something was no longer working (or did not work well in the beginning even) or because someone else informed you that they would no longer be funding the program.

Sometimes failures lead to opportunities. And sometimes successes lead to opportunities. Either way, there is plenty of opportunity when you do not get stuck in the past and instead are looking forward and are open to new opportunity.

Your journey starts with you asking yourself the question, “Do I want to be an entrepreneur?”

And if so, the second question to answer is: “Where do I begin?”

Most entrepreneurs do not know where to start once they have decided that they want to be an entrepreneur. And once they are on their journey, there are many twists and turns along the way—much like the zig-zag diagram I described above—where they can get stuck and need to seek out a mentor who can guide them towards higher levels of success towards making your dream your reality. One thing that is for certain is that you need to continue learning and reading as well as learning from mentors and becoming a mentor to others.
The great thing is that it is possible for you to seek out mentors who can show you the ropes so you can live the life of your

dreams. Some mentors may be people who mentor you directly. Others may be mentors who mentor you through books and audio programs. You can have Tony Robbins, Jim Rohn, Brendon Burchard or countless others mentor you so that you get your mind prepared for your journey as an entrepreneur. It is so important because it will lay the groundwork for you to stay focused so you do not get derailed when you face challenges.

By staying the course, your dream can become your reality. What I enjoy most about being a mentor is that I get to experience the success of my clients with them. Giving them the leverage to become the go-to expert in their field creates those new opportunities to become successful in regards to credibility and profitability.

However, it starts with making the choice to become an entrepreneur and doing what it takes. Although the payoffs are worth it, it does take commitment to make it happen. Having the ability to overcome challenges on the path to success not only starts with self-education and mentoring, these are an integral and continuous part of it.

I have been tenacious about reading. You have got to be reading and reading and reading. The continuous growth is a key aspect of learning how to be successful. Reading is a foundational basis for building a fortune. It is true that there is a place for a formal college education. If you want to be a doctor or an attorney, you need a degree. Other than those types of careers that require a degree, the best advice is to find something you want to do to impact the world—and go for it.

One of my colleagues reminded me of Jim Rohn's quote regarding education, which is something to the effect of the following statement: If you get a proper education through the school system, it will get you a job or a career. If you get a self-education, you will become rich.

That same colleague wisely pointed out that rich can mean financially wealthy, but it can also mean fulfilled.

Sometimes when we start out as entrepreneurs, we think that once we achieve success that that is it. However, you need to bring in other people around you once you reach a certain level so you know what to do to get to the next levels most directly as well as most sustainably.

I know this lesson from personal experience. I reached a level in a business that brought me to a quarter of a million dollars, but it was not sustainable. I found that I could expand some, but I would again reach a certain point. When you reach that type of point, bring in other mentors to coach you to the next levels because different levels require that you think differently and take new actions. You may have some prior experience that provides an analogous experience for you to draw upon so you can understand it from an experiential standpoint. For me, I was able to relate my journey of becoming a successful photographer to my journey as an entrepreneur.

I studied great portrait photographers and translated those lessons learned into my work within the military, where I was assigned to photograph Admirals and Heads-of-State and so forth. I created an exceptional technically correct product for that position. So, as my career evolved in the media, it required me to write as well as to produce and edit video. Through this round-about journey as a photographer within the military, it prepared me for what I am doing now to help others succeed. This mission is what I am supposed to be doing now.

You want to read and apply what works so you can get successful results. As part of your journey, it is key that you continue to read books, reflect on what interests you, reflect on the needs in the market place, find an intersection, specialize, and then micro-specialize. I have become an insatiable reader. You have got to be reading and reading and reading. It is self-education (from reading, learning from mentors, and so forth) that can make you a fortune.

Yes, there is a place for college education if you want to be a doctor or attorney, which requires a degree. Other than in those types of cases, find something that you want to do where you can impact the world with—and go for it! As part of your journey, it is key that you continue to read books, reflect on what interests you, reflect on the needs in the market place, find an intersection, specialize, and then micro-specialize.

That is why *The Authority Code* is a book that provides you with the formula for becoming the authority that can increase your leads, sales and profits.

The book is arranged in 4 Parts to share with you the background of my journey, the benefits of becoming an authority, the code formula components, and the application actions to support you in identifying how to you can customize it for your own authority within your market.

Some chapters in this book are short and some are longer, depending upon what needed to be provided to give just enough description for you to understand the key relevance to my overall journey (which had more zigs and zags than I care to describe) as well as to the authority journey that many people have followed to increase their success so that you can take the same journey—but in your own unique way.

When content in the book sounds repetitious, it is because what is being repeated is very important information. It is also essential to note that there are application ideas that provide the high level actions to take. However, there may be additional actions you may want to take as you customize and apply the formula to your authority-building process. Those additional actions may be ones that are touched upon within the description of another code component section that you want to also apply to some other ones as they are suggestions to consider. To best understand how to maximize your use of this book, it is good to first understand how the content is organized.

Part I – Building towards becoming The Authority is about my own authority journey. My high-level description of my journey describes where I went from challenges mixed with successes in school...that led to photography and media experience within the military...that led to corporate training and speaking...and then finally led to self-publishing for myself and my clients, which has been the high level view of my authority journey for me to finally arrive at knowing that this is where I am supposed to be at the intersection of continually creating my own authority positioning as "The Authority Syndicate" with the mission to serve and support others in establishing and reinforcing their own authority within their market.

Part II – Discovering The Full Power of Authority Status is about the types of success that can result from taking the authority journey that many others have already taken, which can also work for you. This part provides some examples you may recognize.

Part III – Breaking The Authority Code is about how the formula provides an overall streamlined process to follow in creating authority positioning. The entire code has the underlying purpose and theme of creating content and marketing you in the simultaneous process of developing your authority. Ironically, it both compounds and expands your authority simultaneously.

The Authority Code Formula is comprised of 11 code components—including taking actions related to the following individual and collective codes resulting in Authority Positioning: Authority Interviews, Authority Association, News Releases, Best Seller Campaigns, Internet Radio Interviews, Content Development, Digital Magazines, Online Courses, Video Interviews and Speaking Opportunities, Webinars, which can each be highlighted features of an Installed Media Room on your website. I provide you with the highlights related to how these types of actions can help you get featured on Affiliate sites, such as ABC, NBC, CBS and Fox. Having appearances on these types of venues enhance your authority for existing and potential clients.

Part IV – Applying The Exact Authority Code for Success is about your journey of using The Authority Code found in Part III to become the go-to expert in your market.

So, let's get started on breaking The Authority Code...

Part I

Building Toward Becoming The Authority

My Authority Journey

There is always a journey before becoming an authority in a certain area. There may be many detours of becoming an authority in various fields that eventually unite into a grander authority that becomes your uniqueness. This part provides some highlights of my unique journey that eventually lead to my current authority positioning. However, even after you gain authority status, the journey continues...

Chapter 1 - Early Opportunities

As I look ahead to the success that I am currently creating, it requires that I also look back to the history of my journey as an entrepreneur to stay in touch with my passion as well as the lessons I have learned from failures and from successes.

By reflecting, it has become clear how cracking The Authority Code traces back to my early days of entrepreneurial pursuits. Not only was it entrepreneurial—although I may or may not have known at the time that that was what it was called—it involved dreaming, demonstrating leadership, and marketing, among other things.

It was not until decades later, however, that I was exposed to the notion of "authority-style marketing," but from the beginning I recognized that success involves marketing, in one form or another.

As early as 2nd Grade, I remember looking out the window of my classroom. I was daydreaming. I remember thinking to myself, "There's got to be more to life than what they're trying to tell me." Because I was a Daydreamer, I was actually held back that year. Imagine that – I was actually dreaming about a better life even at an early age.

Early on, photography captivated me. I knew that I was going to make a career of it. I grew up around photography because my Father was an amateur photographer. I was amazed by what the process of developing photographs in the darkroom and the outcomes and perspective of what was captured in the photographs.

Because we are now in the Digital Age where photographs are no longer required to be developed in a dark room, many people now—especially of the younger generations—may not be aware of the darkroom.

One thing I distinctly remember about the darkroom was the smell from the chemicals required in the development process. I thought the whole process from capturing photos to developing photos to viewing and distributing photos was fascinating.

It is interesting how interests early on can become a key part of our later success. As you will discover later, I did build upon photography as a central part of a certain phase of my career while I was in the military.

In 8th Grade, I experienced early success as an athlete that brought out my leadership skills. I was a Heavyweight Championship Wrestler when I pinned my opponent in 43 seconds. When I became the City Champ, it was huge for me.

Another taste of success early on was when I was on the winning football team and we became City Football Champions.

Having successes in one area of life early on and later on in life provides perspective to know that you have what it takes to continue to learn, grow and achieve success as a leader and as an entrepreneur.

Marketing for a Market

So, what was that first entrepreneurial pursuit? Well, my first official recollection was when I had a strong desire to enter a river-rafting race, but did not have the money to make it happen—that is, until I created the opportunity...

It was in my hometown area of Indianapolis, Indiana. Every year, the local radio station sponsored a Raft Race down The White River.

I was an eager teenager and wanted to build a raft so badly that I almost could not stand it. The only thing holding me back was that I did not have any money to do it. I thought about what I could do to make money so I could buy the materials to make a raft.

When I put two and two together, I realized that the local grocery store owner who I admired could probably use some marketing. So, I walked into the grocery store and introduced myself. I explained that I would like to enter the Raft Race and wanted to know if he would fund me.

He asked me how it would benefit him. I explained that I would put a sign advertising the grocery store on my raft if he gave me $50.00 so that he would get some marketing as I rafted down the river.

When he agreed and gave me the $50.00, I was hooked. My first marketing deal that I ever did was a win-win!

The desire to enter the race—no matter what type of race or game you pursue—is where it starts because you never know where the journey may lead you.

Marketing as a Photopreneur

Although I am sure I had other entrepreneurial adventures, one of the other significant ones I can recall was related to my passion for photography.

As I mentioned, early on in life is when I made a decision that I was going to be a photographer. I recall having watched my Father capture photos.

As my interest in photography grew, I started studying photography books and modeled my pictures after well-known photographers.

When I connected photography with entrepreneurialism, I knew I really found my niche!

You may be wondering what I did to connect the two – photography + entrepreneurialism.

Well, I secured a photography gig for $500 by photographing a wealthy gentleman's inventory of his home for insurance purposes.

It was my first exposure to being a "photopreneur." It was a milestone discovery. In fact, I still have my business card that promoted my then-business as *Good Image Photography*.

Although my parents were hardworking, blue-collar Americans who worked traditional jobs so they could provide for me, I somehow always envisioned myself running a business.

I also knew there were benefits to going to college that could help land a better-paying job, but I also knew there was other opportunity as well.

Although my career has taken many exciting twists and turns over the years that has positioned my interests and skills to serve others in furthering their own unique authority, it was within those early entrepreneurial opportunities that I discovered the awe of entrepreneurialism—and rediscovered it later in life.

Chapter 2 - School Challenges

While I experienced success outside of traditional learning environments, school was a different story. I was not set up for success in school at all.

Not only was the political climate and school environment during the 1970s turbulent due to active desegregation, there were personal challenges I was having just staying focused and learning within the confines of the classroom.

I had a hard time focusing due to what would now be diagnosed as Attention Deficit Disorder (ADD), but back then there was no diagnosis of the sort.

Instead they would blame students like me for misbehaving instead of being disciplined and focused on learning. They did not recognize ADD; nor did they recognize there are different learning styles.

Not only was it challenging to try to focus on learning, to make matters worse, I was bullied in Grade School.

The gym teacher suggested that if I wanted to fight that I should play football. I pointed out to the gym teacher that I would be glad to play, but that the school did not have a football team.

With these personal distractions in school, the best thing my Mother (bless her heart) did was to take me out of public school and put me in a private school environment that did not have a football team. Even there I had to defend myself, which was why I was always fighting.

My Mother (bless her heart, again) moved me from that school to a different private school that did have a football team. That was the biggest shift in my life. I had the ability to play sports. I had an organized event that I cared about and could participate in. I had low grades because I was more of an athlete than an academic, but I managed to stay eligible so I could play football.

I had coaches around me. They were coaches who cared and had expectations. I got the worst grades in high school because I was an athlete, although I stayed eligible just so I could play football.

The coaches would encourage by saying that I had potential and a chance to go to Notre Dame or a chance to go to Penn State or a chance to go to Alabama, and so on. All of those potential opportunities presented themselves.

In short, football changed my life in school and my life overall for the better.

Chapter 3 - College Football Fumble

So when the college football opportunities did present themselves, I was excited. It was my opportunity to get out of my hometown in search of a better opportunity.

As I was recruited to college and started out on that path to try the college thing, I thought that I would get picked up in Professional Football because I was 6'5" and 260 pounds.

Needless to say, not only did I not get picked up by the Pros, it also did not work out at the college level. In fact, I failed miserably.

I had to make that dreaded call to my Father asking him to send me enough money to return home on a bus. It was a long cross-country bus ride from California back home to Indiana.

I had a lot of time to daydream of a better future while I stared out the window at the cities and the countryside. I just did not know what the better future looked like just yet.

When I got off the bus with bags in hand, it was not long until my Father asked me that question: "Now what are you going to do?"

Instead of viewing the failure with fear, I viewed it as an opportunity to find the next path, the next adventure that may lead to failure in some way—but would be leading me closer to success as well.

By the way—and this point is important to understand—many people are afraid to fail so they never even give themselves a chance to succeed because you have to experience failure in order to get to experience success. So, you need to get out there and fail miserably. Yes, get out there. Fail. Get up. Do it again.

There could have been every opportunity for me to just throw my hands up and say to myself, "I'm just going to have to stay in this little town in Indiana. I'm stuck here just like everybody else working a factory job. Then, after 42 years of factory work (just like my Father did), I will eventually drop dead, never having lived the life I could have lived."

But—

I refused to accept that as what would become my reality.

That is when I discovered an even more exciting opportunity on the horizon with The Navy, where I could not only get out of Indiana, I could get out of the United States and experience The World. This new choice set the course and laid the groundwork for what I was supposed to do with my life.

Chapter 4 - Military Media Service

When I dropped out of college, I heard about there being opportunity to be a photographer in the United States Navy. Although my Father had been in the United States Air Force, he recommended I join the United States Navy.

When I asked him why, he gave me these three important reasons:

1) They have got all the good food.
2) They have got all the money.
3) They get all the women.

I told him that that was good enough for me. So, the next day, I went and signed up for The Navy. The rest is history.

Serving The US Navy Through Its Media

As fortune would have it, not only did I get all of those perks, I also got to put my photography passion to use as I served as a key part of the media for The Navy when I served as "a still photographer" as well as "a motion picture/video cameraman" (a position that is better known these days as "a videographer").

I studied both great photographers and portrait photographers, which I translated into my military work of photographing Admirals and Heads-of-State. I created an exceptional technically correct process and product. So I built on that as my career evolved in media, which required me to write as well as produce and edit video.

I went through all of the advanced training to keep my skills on the cutting edge of technology at the time. For 18 years, I got to have the greatest job ever documenting things for The Navy, including events and situations ranging from Presidential photo shoots to everything in between, such as accidents and so forth.

If it had anything to do with the history of The Navy, I got to document it. Because of the focus of documenting these types of things, I had opportunities to see and document things that people do not normally get to see in their daily life. I got to travel and to see a lot of interesting things around the world. Needless to say, it was a great experience.

My first assignment was to cover The United States President Ronald Reagan during a visit to Honolulu while I was stationed in Hawaii.

I recall how I begged my supervisor to give me that assignment. What can I say except that I was a young and eager Navy Photographer with the assignment to cover him?

When the time came, I was so excited that I got the assignment that I was almost beside myself. When President Reagan was on site at Hickam Air Force Base in Honolulu, I enthusiastically went up to one of his Secret Service Agents; and I said, "I'm here to shoot the President."

I quickly learned (in a matter of seconds, in fact it was) that there was someone else covering The President, too—meaning that that Secret Service Agent and several other Agents like him were there to cover him in a protective way.

My quick lesson began a split second after I finished my statement and that Agent replied to me, "That ain't good, fella."

That is when I found out how quickly they reacted and I went down to the ground. Yes, in my white uniform and all. I was worked over pretty well before I could explain more accurately what I meant.

In the end, I did get the shot off—that is with a camera shot.

Ever since my experience with The Secret Service, I have learned to be especially careful about the way I say something that may have an unintended meaning.

Albeit that I was young and eager at the time, I used the slang meaning of the word "shoot" in photography instead of intending to convey the literal shoot-with-a-gun meaning of the word "shoot" in harming someone physically, let alone The President of the United States.

How that lesson relates to business is that it is important to keep in mind how simple terms and sayings can take on different meanings.

Being an authority means you are a messenger to the world; and as an educator and advocate, it means you have to make sure you are sending the right message.

Before you broadcast your message, it is important to have others look over your message to make sure you are broadcasting the correct message.

So, after that, I had 18 more years of exciting experiences as a Media person, where I was interviewing people, getting people on *Navy News This Week* and on Navy Television.

Being a photographer and videographer allowed me to capture the authority status of President Reagan and other United States' Presidents as well as other Military Elite, such as Heads-of-State and Admirals.

It was great because not only did I get to personally experience lots of exciting opportunities, I eventually grew into leadership and management. I had experienced leadership that had been lying latent since the time of being a wrestling champ. The military opportunities made it resurface, which made a lasting difference in my life not only while I was in the military, but beyond as well.

I became in charge of a division on an aircraft carrier, where I had a $250,000 quarterly budget that I had to manage in addition to being responsible for overseeing 20 photographers working for me.

I recall thinking to myself, "If I can oversee something like this operation, I can do anything." As you know, however, that is not how it works because there is a learning curve—especially when you are operating your own business.

During the last four years in The Navy when I was training recruits, it became especially stressful. If you have ever seen a movie where they have scenes of training recruits, those scenes truly depict how it is—it is that tough for the recruits—not to mention that it is just as tough (if not more so) for the trainers.

It was during that timeframe (approximately 14 years after I had joined The Navy) when I read my first self-improvement book. It was Charles Givens' *How To Super Self You*. I remember it well because reading it was the first of what would become a groundbreaking practice for me to continually read and apply self-improvement and business books.

Although my initial plan was to be in The Navy for just four years, I ended up making a career out of it because, as it turned out, I was in The Navy for 18 years.

In 1998, I retired a PH1 (E-6) Air Warfare/Surface Warfare Specialist a U.S. Navy Photographer and Video Cameraman/Producer. My passion for The Media and News grew out of these experiences.

Transitioning from The Military to Civilian Life is a challenging one that many veterans experience. I was no exception as I went through some challenges that required both some literal and some figurative shifts on my part.

Way back from the early days of when I built the river raft and covered the expenses by marketing for the grocery market, I knew I wanted to own my own business as an entrepreneur.

Although I was an "entrepreneur" while being in The Navy, it was an exceptional opportunity that afforded me the opportunity to develop my leadership and business skills, travel the world, and get paid a stable income while doing what I was passionate about doing.

Although applying my experience in my own business has proven to be invaluable, I did experience the ups and downs of true entrepreneurship *after* leaving The Navy.

Chapter 5 - Trucking Company Shift

My shift into Civilian Life went fairly well, although there was a major speedbump I went over before I headed more directly on my true course. That miniature journey involved a shift-speedbump-shift process as I transitioned into and out of that phase.

Since the last few years in The Military were especially challenging for me being responsible for training recruits, when I had the choice of what I wanted to do, the last thing I wanted to do was to be responsible for anyone (or anything, for that matter).

I went through a 60-day phase of feeling that way. During that time, I was vegetating because that last four-year stint training recruits was the most high-impact, high-intensity job I had ever had in my life. It took a little while for me to de-program and de-accelerate because I was wound up pretty tight.

So when I did finally downshift into a lower gear, of all things, I decided to start a trucking company business that had been on "My Bucket List" ever since I was a child.

Actually how I envisioned it back then was "to drive across the country in a truck."

How I interpreted that dream was by buying a trucking company, which ended up being a nightmare because not only did the business own me, but 9/11 happened.

In fact, 9/11 occurred during one of the first days on the job—so needless to say, it quickly went down hill from there.

I had contracts in Detroit with all the major automobile manufacturers to run what are called "hotshots," which is when I pick up manufactured parts from around the country that have to be delivered to Ford, Chrysler, and GM plants just in time. So it does not stop the production line. It was fairly lucrative before the bottom fell out of it.

There was a moment when I had to make a tough decision. I had gotten to a certain point where I vividly recall thinking to myself, "You know, this is not going to work anymore."

That moment was the "speedbump moment" (that was actually, if the truth be known, in the physical form of a "ditch") that caused me to pause once and for all on the trucking company dream.

It came in Indiana during a blowing snowstorm. I found myself sitting in a truck, with my dog "Kiko" facing backwards in a snowbound ditch, blocking a two lane road. I had 150 gallons of fuel on board. I was not going to freeze to death.

It was at that moment that I said some of the most freeing words when I finally said to myself, "You know, I'm done."

Fortunately, The Military prepared me for the hardships—and eventual successes—I would experience in entrepreneurship. The failure was not all my fault because of the economic environment at the time—but, it took a toll on me.

The great thing is that I had a wonderful friend who told me, "Hey man, why don't you come down to Houston and live in this beautiful home? Just make it yours—and start over."

So, I did. When you decide, something dies and you move forward. There is no shame in making that type of decision.

So, do not be ashamed one bit when you have to make a decision to let one thing go so you can go for another.

If you are not gaining any ground, do not be ashamed or afraid to recognize it and shift gears.

Since 2005 when I made that choice, it has been a rocket ride ever since when I made a final haul to the next major stage of my journey as a Corporate Safety Trainer before the final push towards positioning myself as a Media Strategist who would eventually found and become "The Authority Syndicate."

Chapter 6 - Record-Breaking Corporate Training

The next phase of my journey was in Corporate America. A little while after my retirement from The Navy (and after the trucking company dust had settled), several people approached me to form a company to consult on Safety Leadership Principles.

When I leveraged my skills related to Leadership; Internet and Video Marketing; and Positioning to position the consulting company within the market as the authority on this particular topic, it took off.

I delivered presentations to CEOs of major companies regarding Leadership Skills as they relate to Safety to ensure no one got hurt.

In the mid 2000's, I was the Site Safety Leader for a $300 million dollar project at a major gas and oil company.

Every morning for the year that I was there, it was my responsibility to design a 15-minute topic to present to 1200 employees.

On one occasion, I hired a special speaker to do a presentation for $5,000. Because it was so poorly done, I said to myself, "I can do a better job than that speaker did." So I searched for the best speaker trainer and honed my skills.

Approximately 5 years later, as the Safety Manager and Corporate Trainer for a contractor at a gas and oil company in Texas City, Tx. my team and I hired and trained 1500 employees for a $77 million dollar construction project.

Using the leadership training I helped develop resulted in *1,300,531 work hours over a 90-day period without an injury*. This record that is directly attributed to the training my team and I spearheaded currently stands as a world record for a refinery.

While I was in that position, around 2009 I had a discussion with one of my training partners who happened to be an inventor. He asked me if I knew anything about publishing a book, specifically self-publishing.

I did not know anything, but it piqued my interest to find out more. There was also another person who had self-published his book on deer hunting, which impressed me that he used it as his business card as he gave me a copy. As I immersed myself within the field of self-publishing, I was hooked!

When I published the inventor's first book for him, he was ecstatic! When I saw the excitement on his face as I handed him that book, and the dopamine hit it was priceless—for both of us.

That first experience of helping someone self-publish their book was a key part of what would become the culmination of my current passion and business of positioning people within the marketplace—by publishing their books, producing their podcasts, producing feature articles, and creating News releases, among other means of getting those footprints on the Internet—so they can be found as the leader and authority in their industry.

The ability to position people within the marketplace through publishing and other media-related strategies turned out to be a stepping stone into the next phase of My Authority Journey—yet it did not immediately take shape.

Although I was part of setting World Records and made a lot of money for this corporation, the opportunity came to a halt when one day they suddenly let me know that they did not need my services anymore.

They shut down my 3000-square-foot training facility.

Now that was a major zig-zag reset, which I was totally unprepared to have happen. Even though I had been working on my mindset and other skills such as public speaking.

In fact, it took a while to sink in that they did not need me anymore. Actually it was about 18 months before I was able to bounce back. Even though I knew how important it was to have your mindset set up from the get-go, I was nowhere near ready for that one sudden, major change.

However, little did I know at the time that that change coupled with my new awareness of the power of self-publishing and public speaking would culminate into a major breakthrough for lasting success.

Chapter 7 - Authority Status Breakthrough

Once I did bounce back from the Corporate Training setback, I was able to reflect on my experiences that lead up to me being able to recognize the opportunity before me—particularly since I had the glimpse of success when I published the book and positioned my first client within the marketplace.

When I was handed the self-published book about deer hunting as a business card, it left an immediate and lasting impression on me that I just had to write my own book as well.

However, in my mind, I had already disqualified myself.

This is where you need to get your mindset right before you start to step up because the person in your head is going to start talking to you about why you think you can write a book or whatever it is that you are setting out to do to build your authority.

My mind was saying things like, "You have no business writing a book.... You got C's in English..... You barely graduated from high school..... You played football.... You don't need to be writing a book...." And it went on and on.

If you cannot control your mind regarding these types of thought processes, how can you control anything else going on in as far as building a business?

So, I temporarily talked myself out of actually physically writing a book, but I made it acceptable to do a photo book because I was a photographer, I could do that.

In the end, though, I never did the photo book. I went right into self-publishing books.

I wrote and published a book to claim my authority within the marketplace.

Although the military prepared me for entrepreneurship in some ways, it did not prepare me for how my family would respond when I published my first book.

When I wrote my first book and I presented it to my Grandmother, she looked at me as if I were from Mars—and she was not the only one who had that type of response.

In fact, my entire family was so uncomfortable. They were saying things like, "My goodness. What? You can't do that. What are you thinking about?"

I was nauseous, to say the least—especially because my Grandmother reacted the way she did because I thought it was going to be great for her because she got to see one of her grandchildren write and publish a book.

Instead of being excited and proud, her words were something lukewarm to the effect of "Oh, okay." When I went to visit her just shortly after having published my first book, she actually set it off to the side, which was a physical indication of how she was not interested.

Just prior to the time when she passed away, I went to visit her and was surprised to the point beyond belief that I found my book in an outside box on her porch.

I was in such disbelief that I remember questioning it and saying to myself, "I'm like...Really?"

Be prepared to experience things like that, especially from your family. It happens because even though you start succeeding in any way that they want to see you succeed, you have just separated yourself not only from your competition within your market, but unfortunately from what is the norm and what is expected and accepted within most families because you have exceeded all expectations—and they cannot process it.

As difficult as it is to swallow, that is the truth. I have experienced it myself personally, as I described above.

I do not come from a large family. In fact, I am an only child. I have a lot of aunts and uncles and cousins, but I do not even talk about it around family. They just cannot fathom it.

It has been challenging at times because it has just been an incredible experience that I would like to be able to share with my family, but realize that it is just not worth trying.

Fortunately, even though it was tough to accept this type of response from those that are close to me, I had prepared my mindset. Because I had done so, I knew that it was a possibility to happen.

So, when it did happen, I was able to recognize it more quickly, deal with what was coming up for me as a response to it, and let it roll off. It was very short-lived when it did affect me.

Going forward from those early experiences, I realized that even if it was Thanksgiving that I would not talk about it because nobody in my family was even interested. It no longer affected me significantly because there I knew there was a ton of interest elsewhere—in my true marketplace.

So, when I recommend that you get your mindset right before you delve into being an entrepreneur, I know firsthand from all of these types of non-entrepreneurial, semi-entrepreneurial, and entrepreneurial experiences both personally and professionally that it does take a different mindset than what you have probably experienced before as well as from what formal education teaches you about following the government and robotically doing a job, where a certain high percentage is withheld for taxes.

If you want to impact the world, you have got to leverage your gifts, leverage your authority, and leverage your mission. I cannot emphasize enough that finding the right mentors for the right leverage points is integral to your success.

It is what I have done as well as what all mentors have done to get where they are. Being an entrepreneur can be a journey where you may feel alone many times, yet being a wise entrepreneur means not going it alone so that you have the right mentor providing guidance and support at the right time of your journey.

Using The Authority Code to establish yourself as the authority in your market can help you become successful to such an altitude that you become hunted for your expertise, allowing you to more easily rise above many challenges.

It has taken me over 50 years to figure out what it takes to operate a successful business, but one of the keys that I have learned to shorten the learning curve is to invest in mentors who can guide you towards success faster.

However, the challenges continue...yet you continue to grow and are better- equipped to move beyond them so you turn them into successes.

Part II

Discovering The Full Power of Authority Status

Successful Results from The Authority Journey

As with many types of journeys in life, there are those who have gone before on the journey and paved the way. Although the way has been proven to be a success, however, it allows for variation specific to individual people's own journeys. The Authority Journey is no different in that those who have followed the formula have increased their authority and their success—but in their own way. Discover more in this part about how others have claimed their authority status and what it means when you do...

Chapter 8 - Benefits of Becoming The Authority

When you follow The Authority Code Formula to claim your authority, it makes sense that there will be benefits that will make a difference in your business and in your life. Overall, you can generate a higher volume of leads (where many of them will be higher quality leads); make more sales; and charge more for your expertise that can provide an opportunity to have higher profits. Although you may generate some of the benefits from positioning yourself as an authority, that is only half of what is necessary to more fully benefit from the benefits.

It is equally important that you position yourself to reap the rewards from the benefits because they will not necessarily be within your grasp if you are not well positioned to capture and track the leads that can enable you to follow up with them to make the sales.

Chapter 19 covers more about the overall concepts related to how to do so, while this chapter focuses instead on the potential benefits related to why you want to (and need to) take the authority journey to position yourself as the authority in the first place to set yourself up for increased success.

By taking the steps and achieving Authority Positioning following The Authority Code Formula, it creates a differentiated advantage resulting in a tipping point that establishes what makes you different from your competitors— which, in turn, creates a competitive advantage for you in the eyes of the consumers.

It is important to note that in some “me-too” markets—such as in real estate and financial expert ones—it is more challenging to position yourself as “the authority” compared to your competition because there is so much competition for a more limited market share per capita of quality professionals in the industry.

So, for every person claiming their authority, your responsibility as a business owner is to identify and convey what makes you unique so that your market views you as the undisputed leader and authority. By micro-specializing in a particular niche market within a larger market, you greatly increase your ability to become the authority within your market, which can make even more of a splash so that your exposure can expand beyond your market.

In a nutshell, these are the types of benefits available to you once you take and continue on the authority journey:

- Your authority is what you create based on your expertise using content and 3rd party endorsments
- Your postioning differentiates you from your competition
- Your clients trust you being the leader
- Your clients know you have their best interests in mind
- Your competitive advantage is tipped in your favor
- Your potential clients hunt for you instead of vice versa
- Your business has a stream of new and repeat business
- Your professional fee amount can be increased
- Your leads, sales and profits potentially increase
- Your authority is sustainable by repeating the formula
- Your marketing effectiveness has a compounding effect
- Your dreams can become your reality

By establishing your expertise and then claiming your authority using The Authority Code provides not only a pathway for you to create your authority, but for your market to have a pathway to find you.

Instead of you hunting for others—whether they be authority figures within their markets, potential clients for you, and/or both—you instead become hunted by others who not only want to do business with you, but are willing to pay you higher fees.

When you think about it, though, as well as take into account what the statistics are saying, it really does not even matter how good you really are or how hard you work because only one third of Americans say most people can't be trusted. In fact, a poll administered by *The USA Today* revealed that Americans do not trust one another. That is...until they have what are called "trust triggers," which indicate that the person can be trusted.

If, on the other hand, your prospects do not trust you and/or the fact that you are an authority, to attempt to establish their trust in you and be perceived as an authority, you will have to work 10 times (or more perhaps) as hard to convert them into becoming a customer. Wow! That is a lot of energy involved just to get in the ballpark of having them consider buying from you. If you are fortunate and your prospects DO trust that you are an authority, and the leader then they will pick you over the competition—even if it costs them more money to work with you. That is true positioning power. You can then compound that power over and over as you continue to provide value as well as charge for that value.

When you authentically do want to make a difference for those in your market, your authenticity can shine through, which often translates into higher trust.

Let us consider some examples of highly trusted people. Take Tom Hanks, Sandra Bullock, and Denzel Washington, for example. The media loves and praises all three of them. By analyzing what they have done to be loved and praised by the media is something that you can replicate, if you pay attention to the formula that they have followed.

The key is in the concept "perception is reality." We, as a society and as consumers, have been conditioned to see the media as a credible source of information. Media recommendations influence consumers (aka customers), who give authority to those endorsed by and seen in the media. So, it follows logically and formulaically:

Media talking about you, your product, or your business equals...*credibility* that equals *celebrity* and *instant authority*.

You must generate trust in your market and with the media. When people visit a website, they often look for a trust trigger, which is something that indicates to the potential client that the person and/or the site is the real deal. Derek Halpern is the Founder of Social Triggers. Many times people use testimonials or reviews as social triggers, which are powerful trust triggers. You could also use a picture or include statements with logos, such as:

> "I am a professional who has been featured on NBC, CBS, ABC, Fox, *The Boston Globe*, *Small Business Trendsetters*, *The Miami Herald* and *The Star Tribune*." (Just be certain that whatever media outlets you mention are ones that you have been featured in—and update them regularly.)

Another key thing to keep in mind is that people read 400 to 500 times slower than the rate at which they process images. So you could include your photo; and underneath it, you could include your positioning statement, such as "The Leading Authority of Dentistry."

Getting third-party endorsements beats self-imposed titles and slogans every time. We create third-party endorsements by establishing what is called A Pattern of Authority. Just being seen on some site one time is not enough to establish the level of authority that you are looking for or that you want.

So, it is imperative that you are on multiple authority sites with different headlines and varying third-party endorsements published over a continuing period of time and shared publicly through social media and other methods.

That last statement is profound. You may want to reread it several times to digest it because it is the key to achieving and maintaining your authority.

It is important to follow this motto: "You Do as Authority Does." If you are a published author (or you become a published author), it creates expert status that creates a huge gap between you and your competitors, just as other experts or authority figures have done. What other authority figures do is to take actions similar to the actions outlined within The Authority Code Formula.

By establishing your authority and then maintaining it, the benefits compound and provide you with increase opportunity and success.

Take the authority journey like so many other top experts have done and are doing—so you, too, can reap the benefits.

Chapter 9 - Uniquely "The Authority Syndicate"

With the different aspects of my life and my career, it has provided a variety of adventures and memories that have made my life rich and interesting as well as make my story and my pathway to becoming an authority unique.

Some of those experiences include the ones that I have already covered in Part I related to my overall authority journey to where I am today as T. Allen Hanes & "The Authority Syndicate."

The focus of this chapter, however, is on the culmination of my journey leading me to become "The Authority Syndicate." Elsewhere in this book, I provide other examples of success my own achievements in leveraging my authority as well as that of my clients.

Before I mention more about becoming an expert as "The Authority Syndicate," there are a few additional experiences I want to mention, including calling your attention to the story I described earlier when the Secret Service Agents took me down when I told one of them I was there to "shoot The President" meaning camera-type shooting and not gun-type shooting.
Not many people—if any?—can say they have had that exact experience. (By the way, I would not recommend anyone ever try it either because it did take some hefty explaining on my part before they finally understood what I meant—and I was even in uniform. That shows how serious they are about even a hint at harm coming to The President, and rightly so.)

A couple of other experiences I will never forget are when I was a short-term bodyguard for Dictator Ferdinand Marcos while he was in Hawaii during his exile from The Philippines; and when my family and I survived a volcanic eruption in The Philippines.

Because sharing some of your own life experiences helps make you unique and sets you apart in your market as well, be sure to look back at what types of experiences you could share in a way that not only distinguishes you, but that are shared in such a way that they help others learn something new and/or see new opportunities in business and in life.

Serving Briefly as Dictator Ferdinand Marcos' Bodyguard

When I was moonlighting as a Security Guard in Honolulu, I had a stint where I was a short-term bodyguard for Dictator Ferdinand Marcos when he was in exile from The Philippines.

He was at George Hamilton's beach home. The company I was with at the time got the contract. It was quite the experience.

All that I was armed with as a Security Guard during my shift was a buzzer and handcuffs. However, if something went wrong, all I had to do was hit the buzzer and my backup came in.

My backup included a small Philippine Marine fire team, who were located in the garage. They were all armed with rocket launchers, hand grenades, and more.

Wow! That was an experience. Nothing necessarily happened that required the backup to take full action—but having everything in place just in case created an amazing experience.

What I learned from that experience is that you want to be prepared and on guard at all times as you seek opportunity and protect yourself and others you are responsible to protect.

As you probably know, the military can offer a rich experience. I also learned that it can also be rewarding to have extra opportunities to earn additional money as well as to keep myself busy, which are the reasons why I decided to work a second job.

As entrepreneurs, it is okay if you need to do something else while you build your dream. You see a lot of entrepreneurs do side work, such as driving for Über while simultaneously being very successful building their businesses.

Between the various streams of income, they manage to pay their bills until which time they are able to have their own business cover all their expenses.

The lesson there is to do what you have to do—but still go for your dream. It is part of the zig and the zag of your journey.

Although I was not officially an "entrepreneur" while I was in the military, I already had it in me from those early experiences when I was growing up.

The military did provide me with the ability to have some similitude of entrepreneurial experiences—and having the opportunity to have an additional stream of income and adventure is something that benefitted me later to keep in mind that there are different ways to bring in income when necessary.

Surviving A Volcanic Eruption

I remember it as if it were yesterday, although the year was 1991. The location was Subic Bay, Mt. Pinatubo in The Philippines. For the duration of what was a long 36-hour period of time, my family and the entire Subic Bay Naval Base community (and beyond) experienced total darkness from a volcanic eruption. That alone would have been enough, but there was more...

A super-typhoon hit *simultaneously*! Even the movies about such events cannot capture how overwhelming something like this catastrophic event.

Volcanic ash spewed everywhere, while it was simultaneously raining wet concrete. And when I say "total darkness," I mean the pitch-black type of darkness that prevents you from even seeing your hand when you know for a fact that by the feel of its proximity that it is right in front of your face—but you cannot even see a trace of it. An experience that was truly unexplainable despite my best efforts to describe it!

The entire infrastructure of the area collapsed. There was no food. There was no water. Thank God we had one thing to live off of during that time, which was the soda drink *Orange Nehi* that the troops in Desert Shield had refused to drink that created warehouses full of it because despite their refusal to drink it, it was still deployed there. During such dire circumstances, you never tasted something so good and refreshing—even though it was hot *Orange Nehi* at that.

There were many lessons I learned from that experience. I especially learned that your life can be turned upside down at a moment's notice. It can change for the good or for the bad (and hopefully back to the good...again).

If your entire infrastructure is destroyed like ours was at the time, you have to go back to basics. Quickly, our new priority shifted to have charcoal to cook the food in the fridge before it spoiled.

Once we got our lives back on track after a period of time, I appreciated all the day-to-day things even more—including things that may not be favorites like *Orange Nehi,* yet can make a difference—because having those things helps have a foundation to reach bigger-picture goals that can make life even more fulfilling.

I also learned that when you can survive a temporary setback, especially as extreme as that one was, you prove that you have what it takes to make it through challenges that often come with following your dream and becoming an authority in your area.

Ultimately Becoming An Authority Who Syndicates

By becoming "The Authority Syndicate," it specifically positions me where I can leverage my professional experiences that uniquely and ultimately lead me to this point in time, where I have already demonstrated proven ability to position myself and others as experts.

I had the opportunity to achieve at these levels even before the internet opened opportunities that provided a gateway for everyone.

However, being able to harness the vast opportunity still requires skill and systems—otherwise, the opportunity remains unexplored and dreams remain unlived.

Life is too short to not really live. In order to get to this position, I had to do a lot of resets. The resets are part of the zig-zag experiences that help shape your unique journey.

There are going to be a lot of resets in life and business. Again, there is no shame in having the ability to reset and knowing that it is your God-given ability to be able to do it.

Some of those resets can be as a result of major tragedies that cause you to stop and reflect on what you really want your life to be and what legacy you want to leave behind. From even those types of resets, you come back, calm down, and get refocused.

When my Grandmother, Louella Mitchell Hanes, passed away in 2013, I had one of those major resets. She was a influence on my life as she was for the entire family. She instilled within us a legacy that she handed down to the family. Her legacy is comprised of 7 Principles to live by. Nobody had ever heard of these exact principles, which are as follows:

1) Show kindness to an aged person.
2) Offer the apology that saves a friendship.
3) Destroy a letter written in anger.
4) Stop a scandal from wrecking a reputation.
5) Live complaint-free if you muddy life's water you must drink the dirty water.
6) Accept the judgment of God on any question.
7) Take time to show your consideration.

Because they were so profound, I did a reset. One of my most recent major resets was when I realized that I am on a new mission. It is a new mission to go forward. I am half-way through my life with another 50 years or so to go.

My new mission is that I am going to make a huge impact on the world—and I am going for it. That is why I am driven to continue to mentor and share The Authority Code and other authority-building products I have and will create with others to wake them up to fully recognizing and using their greatness and talents so they can claim their authority, reap the benefits, and start living their dreams!

Chapter 10 - Authority Success Examples

A key part of attaining success is learning. To expedite the time it takes to get through the learning curve, it is wise to find other people who are successful and model your efforts after them—in your own unique way that is.

Not only have these authority-building strategies as described in the chapter on The Authority Code Formula worked for other authority figures (including celebrities), they have also worked for me in establishing myself as an authority by achieving #1 status for my four best sellers and have worked for my clients as well.

Some success examples include Sharon Frame, Barbara Corcoran, Dave Ramsey, Suze Orman, and James Malinchak, to name a few. Although they are success examples I mention here, it does not mean that they followed the exact order of the formula I describe in this book, although they paved their way by having taken similar types of authority-building steps.

There are various related avenues and order of events in which each of them may have taken to initially achieve their success as well as to sustain it. It is notable that their pathways left traces of success that have enabled others to see how they too can achieve authority and celebrity status within their industry.

What happens to be especially great news about The Authority Code Formula as described within this book is the way in which I have streamlined it as a result of not only creating and reinforcing my own authority status, but have followed the same types of steps for more than hundreds of my clients.

This proven track record demonstrates it can also produce maximum success for you in a short as well as a sustainable period of time.

With that said, let me provide some highlights about a handful of the many success examples I have followed as well as some provide some highlights of my own successes in addition to of those I have helped support in increasing their success levels.

Authority Success Examples

Barbara Corcoran

Barbara Corcoran is one of The Sharks on the television program *The Shark Tank*. She became a real estate mogul—although she did not start out that way. In fact, in the book *Shark Tales*, she describes how she started over three decades ago with borrowed money of just a $1,000 investment (the equivalent of approximately $5,000's today). After 33 years, she sold her company for sixty-six million dollars. Not bad for her investment. Along the way, she did some very important things that any entrepreneur or businessperson can do to have the same status authority status within their market.

When she was starting her real estate brokerage firm, she was learning about how to do business. In those early days, she was at an event when she opened *The New York Times*, which had a quote in there from her competitor, who said that the prices of condominiums and apartments in New York City were at an all-time low of $255,000 a property. That quote in *The New York Times* was followed by his name and his company name. Barbara wrote her own two-page report called "The Corcoran Report" about facts and figures about the prior year's real estate sales, which was followed by "Barbara Corcoran of The Corcoran

Group"; and then submitted it to the Editors at *The New York Times*. She became an immediate authority figure and celebrity, who was getting invited to be on television and radio.
When she found out that Madonna was moving to New York and was looking for a condominium. Barbara created "The Madonna Report" to provide answers to questions like: "What would Madonna as a celebrity be looking for in a condominium?" That special report blew up in the media. Barbara got it on TV—and the rest is history.

"How can you pull the rug out from under your competitors? Steal the limelight." Corcoran says she began putting out a regular report on Manhattan real estate to the news media, complete with headline-ready statistics—and before long she was treated as an expert. "The press actually fell for the fact that my people were the power brokers. We weren't!" she says. "Soon I had a new business partner, and his or her name was *The New York Times.*"

A great example of using the authority code!

After selling her real estate business, Barbara leveraged her success to get on *The Shark Tank,* where she continues to leverage her authority as well as find new business opportunities.

My point is that every entrepreneur and businessperson can take those same types of steps similar to what Barbara did to dominate their market. Those steps are the types of steps that comprise The Authority Code Formula consolidated within Chapter 12.

So many authorities have followed a similar path. Because they have positioned themselves as educators and advocates, others view them as such. A huge benefit to that is that they do not need to call themselves the expert nor do they constantly need to be asking people to buy their products and services because they have established a ready-made market who are interested to buy from them over and over again as they develop new offerings.

The great thing is that using The Authority Code Formula you can make these types of foundational breakthroughs to establish yourself as an authority, too.

Other Key Authority Figures

As a financial authority, Dave Ramsey has been in the business for years. A huge aspect of his sustainable success has been due to his micro-specialized focused. He not only helps people who have financial challenges and may even be in the position of going bankrupt as well as needing to start over, he further nano-specializes in talking to Christians who want to get out of debt. He is in every church—and he stays focused on his target market. Another well-known authority figure in the financial arena is Suze Orman who also has a huge following of people who tune in to her programs and buy her products.

In the fitness industry, there are a lot of experts, making it especially challenging to not only breakthrough as an authority, but to remain at that level.

One particular person who comes to mind for a lot of people is Richard Simmons. He is not necessarily the smartest guy in the industry, but everyone knows him and millions buy his fitness information because he is an educator and an advocate. (By the way, if you do not know who he is, search for him on the Internet and you will see for yourself how he is hugely successful because he has positioned himself that way so that he focuses on his target niche.)

Other people are going after the P90X market or the Circuit Fit/Cross Fit trainers. Not Richard. He knows his market. He is going for upper-age people baby boomers; and they identify with him and he identifies with them.

Across the board of various industries, people use speaking as part of their approach for reaching audiences. Within the industry, there are those go-to experts who teach others about what works and what does not within the industry.

James Malinchak is one of those go-to people may not be a household name for everyone, but within the speaking industry, he has positioned himself as a go-to expert for speakers.

Many people have heard of him as having been one of the first millionaires on ABC's first season of the show called *The Secret Millionaire.* The programs he offers share some of the key celebrity-building techniques he and others have used to create their market.

T. Allen Hanes as The Authority Syndicate

The Best-selling Author status has skyrocketed my career as a speaker and in doing what I do. How do you think I got associated with Les Brown where we are both authors of a book chapter in the book I published called *Bold! Helping You Unleash The Hero Within* if I was not first the author of a book? He went and searched if I was a publisher and if I was actually doing what I said I was doing. So, the same approach goes in the small business world.

If someone is going to hire a CPA and somebody else recommends a certain CPA, you can be assured that the person who wants to hire a quality CPA is going to check him or her out. That is, unless they just go on a gut feeling. Generally, however,

9 times out of 10, they are going to check out the CPA by going to Google to search his or her name.

As an expert in your market, you have got to get further than the reviews that most other experts in your market also have. Yes, they are important, but they are not enough to get you positioned as the go-to authority. If the CPA has a book he or she wrote on business taxes with an online presence to that effect, it creates credibility. And if he or she is a Media Contributor on a topic related to his or her expertise (such as "How To Do Taxes") it lends even more credibility.

Having a best-selling book is foundational to creating your credibility. In fact, my first Amazon Best Seller was called *Simple Online Video Marketing for Business Owners*. When I published it, it hit Number 7 in the Advertising category; Number 22 in Marketing and Sales; and Number 41 in Accounting. You only have to be in the Top 100 to be considered a Best-selling Author. However, other books my team has published have hit Number 1, Number 2 and Number 3 in the Top 100 for other books, including for another one of my Amazon Best Sellers called *The Authority Mindset*, which hit Number 1, 2 and 2 in some categories. It also hit Number 1 on the International Best Seller List, which is Amazon overseas in Canada, in Germany, and in other European countries. Achieving that status was not only a milestone for myself, but the fact that I have been able to do the same for hundreds of clients are additional milestones that add to my credibility as The Authority Syndicate.

I also look for opportunities to leverage my authority and celebrity association. In 2015, my first publication in LinkedIn's Pulse section was an article called "How to Start 2015 Like a Shark and Claim Your Authority." In my article, I was talking about

Barbara Corcoran. Every one of my publications is associated with someone famous because it then associates me with them. So I take what I know and I connect it to a celebrity on what they did to get their positioning. I go all the way back to Benjamin Franklin, who was a master at it. Two other authority figures who were also masters at it were former President Franklin D. Roosevelt and Martin Luther King, Jr.

Snapshots of T. Allen Hanes' Client Success

It has been a great privilege and pleasure to serve my clients, who are amazing experts in their markets. Some of them were just starting out and others were somewhat well-known. Each situation differs, but what I can say is that because they can claim their status as "Best-selling Authors" that it has elevated them to a new height that sets them apart from others in their market. Being able to work with them to accelerate and amplify their authority status has provided them with more leads, more sales, and more profits.

One of my mentors for speaking, publishing, and additional media training has been James Malinchak, who was on ABC's first season of *The Secret Millionaire*.

One of my top clients is Sharon Frame, who is a former CNN Anchor.

I have also had the pleasure of connecting with and being part of increasing success for many clients in various markets, including those who I highlight next with Snapshot descriptions to give you a picture of how authority-building has been key for them.

Snapshot #1

One client in particular started out backwards. In mainstream media, in general, you cannot get on TV unless you are a Best-selling Author. It is the first thing they ask you. She called me after the fact. She had not only been on *The Today Show*, she had also already been featured in *People Magazine*. The normal route is that it takes approximately 60 local TV appearances and 100 different markets before you can get on *The Today Show* because when you get there, you have got to be ready-to-go. She got on *The Today Show* and was featured in *People Magazine* immediately. So she rose to fame quickly, yet was not prepared for it.

Delta Airlines asked her to come speak to their employees about weight loss. She had lost about 300 pounds on this program that they created. Delta Airlines asked her to bring her book, but she did not have a book. They informed her that she better get one.

Because my contact with CNN knew that one of my areas of expertise is creating and publishing books, she told her to call me. When she called, she was crying because she did not know what to do. I told her to relax because I knew that we could get her groundbreaking book done in time.

Three weeks later, we had her book published as a best seller prior to when she stood before Delta Airlines talking to their employees. That is the difference. You can create authority and best seller status at the local level. You do not have to wait for somebody to recognize you.

My team and I specialize in doing Best Seller Campaigns. We celebrate the authority with our entrepreneurial authors by giving them nice awards at a special awards ceremony. Then, we publish about them as award winners. The cycle continues from there to create positive authority and celebrity attention around who you are and what you do.

Snapshot #3 – Certified Public Accountant

For example, one of my clients is a CPA, who mentioned that many people have the perception that they can just buy QuickBooks and instantly be an accountant. However, QuickBooks does not adequately explain to a business owner that they may need training. It is like being able to buy a Corvette, yet it does not immediately make you a sports car driver.

I suggested that my client write an article to that effect, which simultaneously informs them as well as positions him as the authority. My client rightfully identified that that type of article could immediately be published in LinkedIn's Pulse section. It requires no waiting to be an influencer, a subject matter expert, or a thought leader.

Snapshot #4 – Construction Company Founder

On your LinkedIn Profile, instead of talking about your product or service, talk about the solution you offer in a quote-type format that is related to an issue that is currently happening.

For example, one of my clients recently founded a major, multi-million dollar construction company. He is particularly interested in oil refineries. One of the top issues there is related to their Union and the safety of the oil refineries. He is an expert in safety.

Because he holds World Records for working safely in oil refineries, it was natural that I encouraged him to combine the two so that he launched his company as well as placed content on his LinkedIn page about his expertise. As a result, he ended up getting quoted on CNN. After that we got him quoted by *Forbes*,

Entrepreneur Inc. and so forth. I also did a complete article in *Examiner* about him.

The great news is that these approaches to leveraging your authority are actions that are ones that I can replicate with all of my clients like you who are experts and want to become the go-to authority in their field. When you go to my quote on *Forbes*, you will find that my focus is to describe what the article is about rather than to tell about what I do.

For example, when I contribute my input in response to the article about people receiving SMS Texts from businesses on how they should respond immediately or they lose, my name "T. Allen Hanes" is highlighted because it is actually a "hot link" to my Webinar that talks about this issue. It is leveraged and accessible through *Forbes*.

Chapter 11 - *Bold!* Authority

One of my five best-seller books is *BOLD! Helping You Unleash The Hero Within*. Although I have already mentioned it elsewhere within this book, it is worth highlighting further within its own chapter because it does require that you take bold actions in establishing and maintaining your authority.

The book was a project with myself and 12 other entrepreneurs—including and The World's Foremost Motivational Speaker, Les Brown.

BOLD! is a demonstration of The Authority Code in action as it provided Authority Association for all of the authors and with the celebrity author, Les Brown. It also reinforced each of the authors' own authority within their own market space.

In the book, all of the entrepreneurs shared about the struggles they had as well as what it took to overcome them. My chapter is called "'Awaken' and be BOLD!" It has been a privilege to not only have my chapter in the book, but to have also received credit as the publisher under my name *T. Allen Hanes Publishing Group*, which reinforces my pen name provided in my other books. It is essential to connect your authority positioning to your name.

By the very nature of the chapter title "*Bold!* Authority," not only did I want to call your attention to how multiple facets of authority positioning can be accomplished with one project or one code component, I also wanted to be sure to emphasize that claiming your authority position requires you to courageously and confidently take "bold actions" as you step up your authority one code component at a time.

In my chapter, I share how important it is that you awaken yourself and realize the gift that you have to give to the world. Your gift is your mission.

This life is not about being stuck in a job working for someone else for 50 plus years. Those days are over. My parents and others dedicated their lives to working in their jobs just to survive. That was all they knew.

However, fulfilling their mission by using their gifts was there in front of them all along—if they had reached out and tapped into it. Making sure that people recognize that they no longer have to settle is part of what drives me.

The great news is that we can not only learn from the successes of others, but also from their failures and missed opportunities.

When you recognize the difference you can make in your market, in your own life, and in the world overall, it builds momentum to continue.

By claiming your authority positioning, it often means stretching beyond your comfort zone so that you have a new, expanded comfort zone in which to operate.

However, when entrepreneurs take new actions to get new results, there can be new challenges. For those times when you may have a situation arise that has you become less than bold and courageous if it presents a challenge, you can do your best to manage it and move on towards regaining the boldness required.

Being an authority inherently calls you to be bold, even if it is a boldness that ranges from being a quiet individual stand for something to speaking affirmatively in a forum. Your opportunities and your brand style will shape how you provide your authority with boldness.

Part III
Breaking The Authority Code
Formula for The Authority Journey

Knowing about The Authority Code and having it provided in a formulaic manner are two different things because the latter provides steps you can repeatedly and predictably follow to increase your success in a sustainable way. By breaking it down, you understand each component code more fully as well as how the codes applied collectively provide the greatest compounding impact in laying the foundation for your authority status in a way that you can continuously build upon it. Seeing the formula as a whole, breaking it down into code parts, and uniting it again into the whole offers a comprehensive way to envision how you can get the formula working for you and what benefits you will gain when you follow this pathway...

Chapter 12 - The Exact Authority Code Formula

Simply the fastest way to get recognized as an authority within 48 hours guaranteed in your market is to follow The Authority Code Formula—especially when you work with an expert who knows how.

Although it takes more than 48 hours to create some parts of the formula, once you get launched by following the formula from the initial stages to completion of the formula steps, your next step is to continue taking actions using the "condensed formula" that increasingly compounds and maintains your authority.

This one formula is comprised of the secrets about what steps to take to position yourself as an authority over your competitors. From that authority position, you can generate more leads, more sales, and more profit.

The assumption is that you are already an expert in your industry, yet may not be known as the go-to authority or not known as well as you would like to be. Another assumption is that you already have a website as a starting place, especially because it serves as a hub for information about you and your business, including that you will have an Installed Media Room as one of the codes within the formula.

For you to position yourself well, as I previously mentioned, it is best to micro-specialize by reflecting on what interests you as well as reflecting on what needs exist in the market place that you could uniquely fulfill. That intersection of "interest + needs" pinpoints where you can micro-specialize.

An important point to recognize is that authority figures do not try to help everyone. It may be cliché, but is so true still today: You cannot help everyone as you cannot be everything to everybody. However, if you are positioned well for your expertise and your passion, you can make a difference and make a fortune at the same time.

To establish an authority positioning, it requires you to micro-specialize. To understand the full power of this type of mindset, consider how many professions, such as in the area of Finance, are overcrowded and it seems like there is little room for you to become the next self-proclaimed expert. Whether you are a Realtor or a Physician looking for ways to differentiate yourself, the principles are the same. The key is to focus on a different and specific niche.

By micro-specializing, you can sharpen your authority within that arena with little to no competitors. Having a narrow focus and expertise enables you to focus even more on solving a specific pain for your target market, which helps you help your customers even better. I cannot emphasize it enough that it is essential to micro-specialize because it creates less competition for authority status. Existing clients will continue to view you as the best so they want to remain your client; and potential clients seek your services, which makes it easier to get prospects commit to doing business with you so that your sales increase.

It does not mean that you will only have business come from within your narrow niche, but that positioning yourself there specifically provides you with abundant opportunity to increase your success level and to make a significant difference for others within that market, which may attract other customers from beyond the scope of your niche.

Being this type of authority creates an unfair reality that levels the playing field when it comes to attracting new customers because it does not matter if you have a college degree; it does not matter how many information products you have bought; and it does not matter how many events you have attended.

However... what does matter is how hard you work as well as what actions you take and those actions that you do not take that you would then waste energy on.

That is why knowing and applying The Authority Code Formula is a huge advantage for you to know what type of media actions to take on a consistent basis.

While there can be immediate results that result from those actions, the true and lasting power is in repeatedly reinforcing and leveraging your authority by taking the formulaic actions consistently, where some that are part of the condensed formula are ones that you will do more often than others.

It is essential to emphasize, however, that the initial time that you go through The Authority Code Formula, it is essential that you complete each code one by one so they lay the foundation for you to build upon. However, it is also important to note that in customizing your own journey that there may be aspects of the formula that you emphasize more than others.

As highlighted in the Introduction, the overview of The Exact Authority Code Formula is comprised of the following 11 Codes that are necessary action steps to result in your desired Authority Positioning:

The Authority Code Formula

AI + 2AA + 3PR + BSC + IR + CON + DM + OC + VI + SP + IMR = Authority Positioning

Establishing Authority Using This Formula

To apply the formula by getting it into action, you must first understand each of its code components. This section below provides a description of each one as well as gives some insight into how they individually and collectively position you as an authority.

Although some of the descriptions are longer than others, it is important to note that the length of the description does not indicate its level of importance as all of them are important in creating the depth and width of your authority as they each compound to maximize and reinforce the authority established. Also, there are a lot of factors involved in making each of the code components happen. It is also worth noting that there are some other areas within this book that provide more information about publishing, marketing, and so forth in building authority. It is beyond the scope of this book, however, to provide detailed, specific how-to steps for each code component, although more details are provided at AuthorityOnFire.com – an Online Course I created to offer additional detailed information about establishing your authority.

Descriptions of The Authority Code Formula Components

Although the ultimate result of using the formula aims to result in your desired Authority Positioning, each code of the formula that you apply along your journey builds toward the Authority Positioning you envision. So, it is essential that you know from the onset what your ideal positioning will be. As previously mentioned, it is primarily focused on your micro-specialized expertise.

AI = Authority Interview

It all begins with an Authority Interview, which becomes an aired recording on the radio where you as the expert are interviewed by a third party, who not only interviews you, but also talks about you. It goes a lot further than you talking about yourself regarding how you are an expert.

Maybe you have met people that say that they are the expert. With authority marketing, you do not have to say that because you have other people who are talking about you, which naturally positions you as such.

I often use The Kardashians as an example. Who has not heard of The Kardashians? Almost everyone has heard of them—even if they do not follow them. They are in the news all the time—and let me tell you that they are not doing anything for the Gross National Product because they are not producing anything. They are basically famous for being famous.

The Authority Positioning for a business owner can produce the same results, but on a positive side. So, when you have third-party people talking about you, it relieves a requirement of you saying, "Hey, look at me. I'm the expert. I can help you." Let your audience tell everybody else.

The Authority Interview is what I also refer to as "The Best Seller Bio" because your interviewer can discuss with you when you first got the bug for being an entrepreneur, how you got started, and so on up to the present day. That is what will be your story.

For my clients, I have a specific set of questions to illicit the information needed. The focus of our client interview is to primarily draw from your story, but touch upon your expertise related to a "one problem/one solution" framework, which is the main focus of an Authority Interview that occurs as part of the Best seller Campaign.

This step is the first one because it automatically begins positioning you as the authority and establishing your credibility. The interview itself is a marketing piece that provides baseline content to produce some of the other pieces of The Authority Code Formula.

2AA= Authority Association

Your Authority Association is a key factor in establishing your positioning, which is why it is important for it to be repeated twice right away from the get-go in the start-up phase.

From the Authority Interview in addition to a short questionnaire, the essential information becomes available from you so you can be featured via articles based upon your interview, which can be published in two authority magazines. One article is in an interview-style format for *Business Innovators Magazine;* and the other article is a feature-story format for *Small Business Trendsetters*.

You will gain some high-powered exposure and association with top experts and celebrities as there are some very influential people on those platforms, where you are also featured. These magazines have authorities such as Dave Ramsey of Financial Peace University, Mark Cuban of *The Shark Tank*, and Jeff Bezos of Amazon.

Having your interview published in both of these venues gives you authority for two primary reasons: 1) you have celebrity association; and 2) you are being published by a third party. The key is being published in a couple of magazines to get started so you are associated with a high caliber of authority and success as a result.

3PR = 3 News Releases

The next step is to have three separate News Releases created and distributed about you. This code component is also repeated right away from the get-go in the Start-Up Phase because it also helps lay the foundation for your authority.

The three News Releases inform The News of the events that happened positioning you as an authority, namely 1) your Authority Interview as featured on the radio; 2) your article published in *Business Innovators Magazine*; and 3) your article published in *Small Business Trends*.

Each News Release is syndicated to online affiliates of NBC, CBS, ABC, FOX, where approximately 100+ other affiliates receive it—all in one swipe!

Even at this point—prior to moving through the other Authority Code components—you could get featured on TV in your local area. My team and I can show our clients how to be able to leverage that Media towards generating other TV appearances in addition to other forms of Media as well as how to quickly move through the other steps of The Authority Code Formula.

For our clients, we spin the two articles and their related News Releases so they have the same core content, but with a different spin that makes the article unique enough, yet consistent with your overall message. We appropriately use first-person and third-person pronouns and language so that we spin these stories based on the original information provided.

As emphasized previously, throughout relevant parts of The Authority Code Formula, you want to continue to generate News Releases to announce to The News your recent events. In essence, you are creating news.

It is also important to note that because the general purpose behind many of these actions is to get publicity that—even if it does not refer to submitting a News Release (which is itself one of the codes)—you should always ask yourself "Is this newsworthy?" And if so, submit a News Release to keep The News informed.

To once again use The Kardashians as an example for creating news, they have used various approaches, such as "Let's-leave-my-kid-in-the-lobby-of-this-hotel-and-see-if-The-Media-picks-it-up-on-the-news" approach. It is intentionally designed for attention-getting.

I am sorry to reveal this news to you, but that is how it is often done to intentionally create news for people and for businesses in The Media.

If you are waiting to see if they are going to come and contact you—unless you pull a crime off—you need to think again because they are not going to seek you out and talk to you. Bad news is not as good as good news. So, all the noise is talking about creating news—legitimate, good news. As you go along, create good news and let The News know!

BSC = Best Seller Campaign

So, why is being a Best-selling Author so valuable? Well, here is what happens as a result. It gets other media to pay attention. You have a book. You will possibly be asked to appear on television. You will be asked to speak. It creates a building block to fuel demand. There are a variety of venues, such as radio, speaking engagements, TV, etc. When you get introduced by statements such as "Please welcome Best-selling Author" followed by your name, it also gets other media to pay attention. You start getting asked to appear on radio shows and being interviewed. All of that media attention further creates authority.

You may be saying to yourself, "That's great news about authority positioning, but I don't have a book." Well, the even greater news is that entrepreneurs can become Best-selling Authors without having to write a book themselves. With a book, you position yourself as an authority. People looking for the types of products and/or services you provide pick you instead of your competitors because of the credibility having a book provides. So, having a book could result in you having more leads, more sales and more profits.

So, let's define a best seller. Well, there really is no official legal definition. You are probably familiar with the notion of a Best Seller List. Generally, if an author is ranked in the Top 100 of a recognized Best Seller List as determined by each list type offered by the Publisher, it is considered a best seller. For Publishers who provide Best Seller Lists, you have got *The New York Times*, *The Wall Street Journal*, and Amazon.com, which is heaven-sent for entrepreneurs. So, becoming a Best-selling Author by organically marketing and selling books is a great achievement. Authors have been buying their way onto the Best Seller List for years. I am sorry if you are disappointed, but that is the truth. It is a very common practice.

Dr. Bill Dorfman, who is the dentist to The Stars and also runs LEAP, a leadership foundation for children, had his best-selling book campaign when *Extreme Makeover* came out. He was already a billionaire when he sent his book to 9,000 of his clients because they were buying product from him every month because he was distributing a teeth-whitening product that he invented. He instructed all the people that he sent the book to to buy another one, or to give one to a friend. So, that was approximately 18,000 books. For *The Wall Street Journal*, it takes about 3,000 copies to ensure a spot on the Best Seller List. For *The New York Times*, it is approximately 9,000 copies to ensure a spot on theirs.

I am about to expose a little-known and rarely talked about "loophole" that has been used by many business leaders to become Best-selling Authors and authorities within their market, even if their book is a complete flop. It is not about selling a lot of books. In fact, it is exactly the opposite. It is about becoming a Best-selling Author in spite of not selling a lot of books. So, here is the loophole: The New York Times' list of best-selling books is evaluated or updated weekly. For Amazon.com, on the other hand, the best-selling books are updated hourly. That creates a loophole.

Based on our proven strategies for positioning the Kindle book, we guarantee it will become a national best seller in at least one categorie—and possibly international best seller. For the Amazon Best Seller ratings, you have to be in the Top 100. Our clients' books usually hit Number 1, Number 2 or Number 3, however. With other interviews, you can also create other Kindle books.

Having other Kindle books provides other displayed digital products that compound your expertise. For some of the topics, you can review your experiences or you can review generalized client cases you have worked on to identify what types of problems are common and how to solve them.

So, not only have we proven we can help people like you get published, we have also help them become Best-selling Authors that skyrockets their authority.

Although this code is a “Best Seller Campaign” that does not explicitly have the word “published” in it, it implies that you publish a book as part of establishing your authority status. Being a published author is a key step in positioning you as an expert. The word “author,” which specifically means “originator who gives something existence,” itself is the first part of the word “authority.”

This code is a 4-step process that is focused on creating and implementing a campaign, which includes: 1) getting the book done; 2) getting it published; 3) getting it launched to the best seller status; and 4) getting The News informed of that status. As you can see, some of these codes have their “sub-code” steps as well in order to accomplish the higher result of achieving the code.

Many people have a lot of expertise, but one of them may not be in the area of writing. The good news is that my team and I have other techniques where you can create a book with your words and ideas, yet someone else does the actual writing for you—so you do not even have to write a word.

To create your Best Seller Campaign, the Authority Interview not only provides content for the two articles, it also provides the baseline content to create a 4,000-word Kindle (digital) book. This interview-based book is an entry-point book to initially position you as being a published author. Being published itself is a major milestone that is admirable; but when I position books so they become Best-selling Authors (and often times International Best-selling Authors), it immediately raises the authority status of my clients. (Refer to Chapter 14 for additional information on publishing and Best Seller Campaigns.)

Becoming a published, Best-selling Author is one of the fundamental steps that provide the opportunity to be the go-to authority. There are other parts of The Authority Code Formula that then further reinforce their authority status.

What is exciting is that the opportunity is unlimited because you can write as many books—digital and/or print versions—as you want on your expertise. Once we get you Kindle-published, we take you to best seller status and leverage your new positioning so that you will be introduced as a "Best-selling Author" forever.

Once you become a Best-selling Author for the first time with a Kindle book, we go back to the phase of you being the content creator, the educator, and the advocate. You must be providing content to educate your market, which, again, is especially important for you to micro-specialize so that you know who your target market is as you create content for them.

In the start-up phase, you become a published author with two magazine articles about you, which can then expand your exposure that can result in having additional articles published about you in major media outlets, such as *Entrepreneur*

Magazine, Inc., Business Insider, The Wall Street Journal and so forth. Once you are a Best-selling Author, it can help you in increasing your leads, sales and profits—if you position yourself to continually leverage that success.

IR = Internet Radio

Being interviewed on an Internet Radio Show and/or having your own Internet Radio Show is an excellent way to be the expert or authority. There has never been a better time to host your own radio show and get your message out. You can continually compound your expertise.

It is basically the same concept as what was previously better known as the "Podcast." Be careful, though, how you use the term "Podcast" because it is dated since it refers to the outdated technology of the iPod, which most people do not have around anymore. Instead, people carry around various types of smartphones that have multiple capabilities.

Having your own Radio Show via the Internet as well as being a guest on other people's Radio Shows is an excellent platform to promote yourself as an authority based on what you do to serve others. Having a position of service enables you to connect with your audience as well as potentially grow your following.

My Radio Show is "The Authority Syndicate Radio Show," where I talk about the experts and bring people on my show like you, which gives you a piece of digital landscape. During the show, I talk with my guests about how to relieve a problem in their market and use that to distribute it out. Being a guest on my show provides them with an opportunity to "Wow!" their market because they were interviewed by "T. Allen Hanes, The Authority Syndicate."

In addition to being my guest, we teach you how to get on other similar types of shows. It literally just depends upon how much time you have because there are people begging to get you on their shows. These interviews can then be transcribed and leveraged as other written content for articles and/or books, depending upon the type of agreement you have with those people who interview you or who you interview. The various code components reinforce and build upon each other as you continually become an educator and an advocate.

CON = Content

As an authority, it cannot be emphasized enough that you have to be an educator and an advocate for your target audience, which means that you provide value through the content you create. Content and marketing relate to all of the code components.

All of the various forms of code components in one way or another fit into the category as being "content," which contain information that conveys your expertise to your market. The purpose of Content is to provide value, interact, and serve your market so that a byproduct of that purpose and focus is to also increase your sales and income. However, it is a good idea to still have a specified code component that specifically refers to "content" so that it calls attention to the importance of always creating content related to your expertise within various content forms as well as to stay relevant.

This particular code component also refers to building content specifically on your website as well as through social media platforms so that figuratively speaking you are building "across the board" and across the internet a consistent content base that is innovative across various platforms. It is also essential for you to also identify the types of information that relate to your area of expertise so you are consistently communicating the vital information about your field and your expertise to your market. The content is both serving your clients in making a difference for them while simultaneously marketing you and your services.

Your core content can be conveyed through audio, video and written formats, including books, articles, blogs and so on that are part of a consistent messaging that brands you as an authority. Your content can be distributed online via your website, through traditional Media platforms as well as Social Media ones, including via LinkedIn, Medium.com, *Entrepreneur*, *HuffPost*, YouTube and so forth.

The content of your content needs to stand out from the crowd, which means for it to be noteworthy it must be fresh, relevant, and relieve a pain in your marketplace.

Just consider how you yourself would go about finding the authority in a particular market for some important service that you need. If you need someone to help you relieve a pain, what is the first thing you do? You ask your inner circle for someone.

For example, if you need someone to remodel your kitchen, you get a name from your church or your friend. Then, you immediately check him or her out by going to Google. That is just how it is. Even employers now do a search on you. What are they going to find? Maybe a LinkedIn account that has not been updated recently. Maybe a couple of Yelp reviews that are only 3 stars.

But as they are looking, they may find another local contractor who has an array of authority that results from the type of authority-building actions promoted within this book. So the other local contractor may have the following types of authority content indicators through various forms of media:

- Providing regular contributions to LinkedIn Pulse
- Providing video content on his own YouTube Channel telling you how to remodel your kitchen
- Providing latest tips and strategies in a best-selling book
- Providing contributions to *Do It Yourself Magazine*
- Providing do-it-yourself techniques via their own magazine
- Providing interviews on Internet Radio Shows
- Providing information to viewers as covered on ABC, CBS, NBC and FOX

With a consistent online presence such as that with authority across the board, who are you going to pick?

Most likely, you said that you would choose the one with the most perceived authority. That is the reason that you, as the expert that you are, need to take the authority-building journey based upon The Authority Code Formula.

The various forms of content must have a consistent message related to your brand, yet with uniqueness and variation that also complies with the style and confines of the particular outlet you use, such as through your Website, YouTube, Twitter, etc. that each have distinct frameworks and norms.

Content within your Website, LinkedIn, & Social Media overall

Your website is vitally important for you to preliminarily have it set up for success prior to applying The Authority Code Formula as it is a foundational location to unite your information, products and/or services as well as your Media within your Media Room.

Once people visit your Website, they will generally go directly to your LinkedIn Profile to make a decision if you can help them. So, your LinkedIn Profile is equally important.

If you are not utilizing LinkedIn properly, you are losing business because that is the big blue ocean of opportunity right now. It is where you should be making all your deals, if not face-to-face.

Your LinkedIn Profile content is very important to establishing and maintaining your authority, which is why your Profile Summary must be an All-Star Summary set up to explain how you help people. In fact, it is probably going to be all over inaudible business. The magic of LinkedIn is that it connects you with those people you need to be engaging with and targeting.

That is the reason the summary section on your LinkedIn Profile has to be positioned just right. Rather than following the traditional format that LinkedIn Profiles generally provide—such as describing who you are and what you do well within your resume or instead of talking about your product or service—highlight who you are and the results you provide in the form of a quote format that describes your mission and the solution you offer that is related to a current issue that relieves pain within your market.

My LinkedIn Profile focuses on how I help you be recognized for your expertise by using my authority-building and Media expertise strategies. It particularly appeals to those people who may not want to do all the details.

Your LinkedIn Profile could also provide all of your information in your summary, including all of your articles that you got picked up on. If potential clients ask you about your past projects, your current projects, your publications, your awards and so forth, it all starts to compound.

With the Basic on LinkedIn, you can display this type of summary, although you are limited to how many people you can see who have viewed your summary. Although the Basic Level only allows you to see five people, I selected to invest in my business and be at the next one up, which is the Premium Level, so I can see whoever looked at my LinkedIn Profile, which is critical because those are leads. What is great is that LinkedIn is the only platform where you can connect with somebody that looked at your profile, yet had not taken any action. When I follow up on those LinkedIn leads, here is the giving-mode technique I use and recommend that others use when someone connects with you:

- I immediately provide them with a brief message thanking them for their time as well as expressing how I appreciate them checking out my profile.
- I let them know that I will be happy to help in any way I can with your business.
- Then, I say, "Oh, by the way, here's a copy of my #1 International Best-selling Book with Les Brown. I'd love for you to review it and provide your comments. You can download it here." (The word "here" is what is hyperlinked to where they can download it.)

From being in a giving mode—which I enjoy doing—I get the added benefit of so much coming back. People indicate things such as, "Wow, you're the only person who has ever given anything. Most people always hit me between the eyes with buy this or buy that."

So, the key is "to give," which opens doors to developing relationships. It is important to consistently have this approach with everybody. It is also important that you have a book in the first place in order to be able to give it away. Once you have various books, you can choose which one to give away.

After you have established yourself and separated yourself from your competition within your market is when you can then utilize Whitepages and Reports to build content that moves you forward. There is even an automated way I have of contacting people. It is so powerful that it goes through all of the gatekeepers. In fact, I could not keep up with all the contacts and had to shut it off.

For this type of connection, my message may be something such as:

- Hi. I would like to connect with you because I looked at your summary; and I think we would be a good fit.

Because the opportunity on LinkedIn is so vast, you must know your ideal client. Go where they are and seek out the groups your ideal client is most likely to be found within. Because they are talking to each other somewhere, you do not want to go into a group to see what you can get from being in the group.

Not only continue to be within your giving mode, you also want to stay within the targeted groups that relate to your expertise. If it is too general, such as within a "marketing group," avoid such groups because everybody is there doing what you are doing.

Instead go into a group that can use your services, such as in groups for entrepreneurs, small business owners, start-ups....

It brings us back to the key point and reason that you want to micro-specialize in the first place, which is because then you know who your market is as well as how to target your message specifically to them.

If you connect with me on LinkedIn by visiting my website tallenhanes.com, it redirects you to my LinkedIn platform where you can message me about sharing with you some additional information that is too valuable to share in an open forum. I will also send you 5 daily tactics to get your phone to ring by using authority marketing.

An important approach to getting noticed by the media is known as "NewsJacking," which is when you attach your authority content to something that is going on in the news. A secret tip is to first share it on Twitter; and then from Twitter use the "Add LinkedIn" button on there. When you do add LinkedIn, click "Pulse" when you get to the end of it. By doing so, it gets the attention of the Pulse Editors, who could take that story and place it into a bigger category pool. Mine often get picked up on *Entrepreneur* and *Small Business Trends*. There are 10 million people located there. In fact, I have made it 5 out of 7 times using these types of methods. More people see your article using these techniques. We have had articles getting up to 50,000 views. Once you connect with me via LinkedIn, there are some additional techniques I can share with you outside of a public forum.

I did a NewsJack with the Super Bowl when everybody claimed that the Seattle Coach made a bad call. I titled my publication "Three Things Entrepreneurs Must Know When Making a Bad

Business Decision." Then, I merged it. You can immediately start positioning yourself as an authority today by publishing on LinkedIn's Pulse. It is important to know that there is a right way to do it. You want to come from being an educator and an advocate. Remember that you are not selling. Any content you create to be published in these types of venues cannot be about selling. It cannot be emphasized enough that instead, it is about educating—regardless of if people pay you or not for that information.

When you are on LinkedIn, you have the option of posting or stats. When you select "Post," it opens up and places you at the Pulse format, where you do your articles. At the bottom of your articles, be sure to copy my format so that you always say, "Thank you for reading my article. If you could 'Like, Comment, and Share it.' I would appreciate it." Then, I have a logo that says, "Thank You." After you connect with me on LinkedIn, go to my content page and find the publication called "Model My Articles," which will provide more details about what to do and not do.

In addition to LinkedIn, the various other forms of Social Media—such as Facebook, Twitter, and so forth—can be included as part of the CON code as they do not necessarily require a code of their own within the formula, although they individually reinforce the foundation that is established as a result of the overall authority-building actions highlighted by the formula.

Social Media provides opportunity to engage with your market to provide value as well as to occasionally mention Humble Brags. With the various forms of Social Media, it is important to know the differences of the venues as well as to be in a giving mode rather than a selling mode.

Based on the various forms of social media as well as content that is authority-building using techniques from The Authority Code Formula, you can increase your Google rankings so that your name is attached to the various forms of authority you are building.

Another related avenue is to write stories to help people understand what it is that you believe in a compelling and persuasive manner. When you bring all of that together, you get asked to appear on television, to be included in books, and to speak to industry associations and conferences. Each of these opportunities are the tipping points.

You can see how quality content in various forms is key to communicating your message, marketing your expertise, and making a difference.

DM = Digital Magazine

Just as is the case with the Internet Radio, the Digital Magazine is another substantial way to establish your authority by being a contributor to an existing Digital Magazine and/or becoming the publisher of your own Digital Magazine. It is an awesome way to simultaneously positioning yourself as an authority, an educator, and an advocate.

The reason it is especially important to create a Digital Magazine is because in the past, people and organizations had newsletters to keep their market informed and engaged. Today, Digital Magazines are replacing newsletters. What is especially great about it is that it gives you lots of prestige when you are the publisher of your own.

It is easy to publish one because you start by getting some slick graphics, which is easy to do because you can buy a template online. You can publish and distribute it free online. However, you may decide to charge for it, if you like. The content from some of your interviews can also be leveraged and reframed in a variety of ways for articles. I provide a platform with all the authority people I do interviews with as well as offer the opportunity to create magazines for them.

OC = Online Course

When you work individually with various people and customize your services specific to their situation, there are always some generalities that emerge that need to be consistently done so that people get the results.

By streamlining the information via an Online Course as well as providing some customized information to demonstrate how the information you provide can be tailored in some situations, you can create another product (aka your Online Course) that will both expand and deepen your authority positioning as well as help even more people.

Having an Online Course provides an exceptional opportunity for you to be the authority while you are able to go deeper into providing value in a systematic way, where others can learn from you. It is beneficial because you can create it once and sell it over and over as a product that provides background knowledge as part of your overall service. Different courses can have different purposes. So, it is important to know what outcomes you want to achieve as you design the program. As part of your course, you can use a combination of audio, video, images, templates, etc. These can also be transcribed and leveraged to create other content.

One of my products is my Online Course (also known as an eCourse) called The Authority Academy, which provides you with additional information about how to establish your authority. Go to AuthorityOnFire.com for more details about what it can do for you.

VI = Video Interview

Video Interviews are great for various reasons. My team and I do a Video Interviews (VI) that is in an interview format, which is often conducted by my client Sharon Frame, a former CNN Anchor. When people search for topics related to what you offer and they find you over and over again across various venues, you increasingly become the go-to expert. Videos are especially great because people connect with you even more. Videos also provide for content creation as well as for online courses related to your books.

Once you position yourself as an authority in your market, you can look for additional opportunities, such as becoming a Weekly Contributor to a Major Media Network, which can get you great positioning. As your name is searched, your articles and videos come up high in the search results of such Video Sites.

Your focus in this type of Media outlet is to share your expertise in helping others relieve their pain. It is imperative, though, that you share within a journalistic format rather than in a selling format. If you even have a hint at selling, you could be banned from their site forever. I have messed that one up a couple of times.

Over the years of practicing, I learned the hard way by having two articles removed from CNN—but have since figured out how to share without making those mistakes. If it is USA Today Video Site, CNN, USA Today, BuzzFeed, or any other Major Media Network, the rules about avoiding any hint of selling apply. These various venues provide additional tools to position your stories in a way that expands your audience while enabling you to share your expertise.

There is a lot of opportunity available—especially when you apply the "News Jack Strategy" that was previously mentioned elsewhere within this book, which is basically when you tie your expert input via a quote you post to a story that is actually already in the news. The Media may pick up on it and contact you for an interview.

SP = Speaker

Speaking in any format is a form of speaking. However, when you speak in front of a live audience, you are able to engage them in a way that provides an opportunity for them to connect with you that differs from how they may connect with you in other formats, such as through radio, television, webinars, audio recordings, and so on. Each format has its pros and cons, which is why it is ideal to utilize various speaking modes of getting your message out.

So, it is another great way to reinforce and expand your influence as an authority is through speaking. Some opportunities may be ones that you are invited to participate in, such as being a speaker at a local Meetup; while other ones may be opportunities where you are creating your own Meetup or other type of event. I started speaking in Corporate America. Later, I joined the Public Speakers Association as a Director so I could lead my own Chapter and be positioned in the community as a Leader. The interviews and other forms of content provide you with a variety of content related to your expertise that you can leverage as a speaker. Chapter 15 has additional information specifically related to the role of speaking as an authority.

IMR = Install Media Room

By following my programs, specifically The Authority Code Formula as outlined within this book, it can take you all the way to television. When you get to that level, you will have television clips that you can include in your website's Media Room.

Most likely, you probably already have a website. If you do not, it is essential that you have one. And if you already have one, it is essential that you are using it effectively to inform and engage your market in a way that they want to stay connected with you as you grow your influence and business.

Your website is a foundational platform that connects the various types of media you are generating. A key part of your website is to do what is called "Install a Media Room" so that you can showcase your authority not only to your market, but also to the other Media who may be interested to find out what else you have done. Within your Media Room, you can include links to various types of publicity you have, such as links to your Interviews, Blogs, Radio Show Interviews, News Releases, Digital Magazines, and so on.

As you build a foundation for your authority, the links to your Interviews, Articles, News Releases and so forth each located within an established Media Room basically provides you with a Media Page, which is searchable by your name so that other Media can find you. Each time you have additional content and/or media, the Media Room is where you drop your links to your books, your articles, your third-party publications, your video clips of TV, your video and so forth.

In short, as you generate various forms of media surrounding your authority, it is important to keep your Media Room on your website updated so that The News is informed and your market is educated about who you are and what you do will have one centralized location to be able to access the various media forms that create and reinforce your credibility.

Authority Positioning

When all of these code components come together, they establish you as the authority. It is important to go through the entire formula without missing a code along the way—but it does not stop there because that is just the initial foundation. It is important to consistently do repeat these steps with variation consistently over time in a way that brands you and the name you are making for yourself.

As you can see, the combination of these codes that represent a multifaceted action-step formula is challenging to achieve without having the support of an expert who knows how to effectively utilize The Authority Code Formula.

However, you can certainly create these opportunities for yourself, although learning the how-to's of connecting with The Media outlets, finding all the magazines to contribute to for your area of expertise, getting interviewed, writing your book, producing your content and publishing it, and so forth requires a massive learning curve in order to implement them effectively and in an order in which they compound upon each other.

You have to decide if you want to wait three years (or maybe never) for The Media to come talk to you, which is highly unlikely. Or, you can compress time to three months or sooner so you get the recognition you deserve. If you do it or if we do it for you, either way, it is a lot of work. However, because we have worked diligently to set up a system, we can streamline it and do it for you so that you get the benefit of the results sooner than later.

Once you establish the foundation of your authority platform using The Authority Code Formula, to keep it strong, you need to continue to maintain and reinforce it using the condensed version of the formula as well as regularly considering how to apply the overall formula, which involves some lengthier projects, such as books and online courses that are not as easily created on a monthly basis. So, the condensed version builds constant momentum with shorter pieces of content and marketing activities in the interim. The next chapter covers more about the two phases of building and maintaining authority. The application of both of these phases is also emphasized with specific actions in Chapter 18 that is organized according to first establishing your authority using The Authority Code Formula in its entirety followed by the condensed version of applying it. With each step, your authority compounds in an exciting and fresh way as you provide value and stay relevant to your target market.

Chapter 13 - Phases of Building Authority

Now that you have an understanding of what component codes comprises The Authority Code Formula, it is important to emphasize that the entire formula needs to be followed for the initial start-up phase (which is the first-time run through of applying the formula) as well as needs to be repeated for the ongoing maintenance phase.

For the latter, you will continue to repeat the steps that focus on your core message(s), yet in a fresh and relevant manner respective to what is happening in your market and in the world.

The point of this chapter is to basically reinforce that there is the first, getting started phase—and then the ongoing phase that goes on and on and on throughout your authority journey that is a pinnacle phase of the career you as an entrepreneur are creating.

So, it is important to emphasize that this is not a one-time set of actions because it is a journey that continues to compound and reinforce your authority.

In fact, the maintenance phase of applying the condensed or "shorthand" view of The Authority Code Formula is to be maintained every month so that each step is done consistently and with enough frequency.

However, it is best to refer regularly to The Authority Code Formula you applied in the Startup Phase to ensure that you are maximizing all that it has to offer as you customize it to build your authority as some of those other codes need to be applied again as well.

For ease of comparison, here are the two versions of the formula:

The Authority Code Formula
AI + 2AA + 3PR + BSC + IR + CON + DM + OC + IMR + VI + SP = **Authority Positioning Established**

The Authority Code Formula [Condensed for Monthly Repetition]
AA + IR + BSC + PR + OC+SP = **Authority Positioning Maintained**

Chapter 18 provides application activities related to applying both the full and condensed version of the formula for the Startup and Maintenance Phases in order to provide you with suggestions to point you in the direction of what types of factors you need to consider as you implement the steps for the codes.

Over time—as you grow and develop more personally and professionally in addition to ways that the market and the world change—you will adjust in some ways, yet hold true to certain timeless principles in other ways.

Since it is based on fundamental marketing that works, The Authority Code Formula will basically stay the same as well. However, there may be some changes over time, such as has been demonstrated from changes involving references to Traditional Radio to Podcast to Internet Radio, although each of them are still currently used to varying degrees.

The difference that will always exist for this type of powerful authority-building marketing described in this book, however, is that it portrays you and what you do in a highly elevated manner that manufactures authority.

With both the initial start-up and maintenance phases, it is essential that you carefully consider how you are intentionally creating your authority and how you are serving your market, which is reciprocal in their relationship to one another.

As you publish, speak, and market, you have opportunity to provide value and serve as well as compound the impact of your authority-building actions.

Moreover, when you keep in mind how to utilize your expertise in the service of others, it creates a natural and genuine demeanor that complements your authority, which can draw others to want to work with you.

To Schedule a No Obligation Authority Breakthrough Session
To learn more about "The Authority Mindset"
Additional video training is available at
www.theincomparibleauthority.com
or www.claimyourauthoritynow.com

Chapter 14 - Publishing as The Authority

One of the most important components in establishing your authority platform on a widespread basis is to publish a book—not only one book (although that alone could differentiate you), but publishing multiple books.

These are two basic parts of the publishing equation:

(1) Creating a book.
(2) Getting it published.

Having a published book does not in and of itself create authority, however. You have to add a third emphasis, which is to market yourself and the book strategically, including targeting the outcome of becoming a best-seller.

Because publishing, speaking and marketing are distinct, yet integrally connect, it is important to have a chapter on each of them, where this chapter focuses solely on how essential publishing as the authority is to your increased business success.

With the first book that I published, it was a breakthrough because prior to that I recognized I had the marketing background, but needed the self-publishing. The breakthrough of publishing that first book for my first client created an opening for me to add another layer of my professional background that provided a well-rounded foundation for me to support myself and others in this arena.

I recognized the power of publishing, but had disqualified myself from ever being an author. It just was not within the scope of what I saw within my mind as possible for myself. Up until that moment, that is. That is why I also emphasize the importance of reading and having mentors so you are getting your mind prepared so that you do not talk yourself out of doing what is possible for you to do. Before this empowering interaction with him, my thoughts repeatedly reinforced negative ideas, such as: "You have no business writing a book. You got C's in English. You barely graduated from high school. You played football. You don't need to be writing no book." That type of tape would play over and over in my mind. No wonder I had never written a book before with those types of thoughts limiting my opportunities. If you cannot control your mind from being focused on these types of negative thoughts, how can you control anything else as far as building a business? Although I knew I needed to control my thoughts, early on, they still controlled me to a large extent, which is why I talked myself out of actually physically writing a book with words. However, I made it acceptable within my mind to do a photo book because I could justify that I was qualified for that type of book since I had substantial experience as a photographer. The interesting thing is that I never did the photo book. Instead, I delved right into writing books. That was not only a transition, it was a leap. You could even call it a personal reset.

- Now, I'm a writer and a publisher. Who would have thought that I would be doing this 35 years later? So, anybody can write a book about your expertise because you are the expert. It is just about packaging your knowledge in the form of a book.
- Being published brings ongoing opportunities and benefits that cannot always be predicted.

Similarly, in your particular niche, you may also find other areas open up that you cannot currently see. So part of success is keeping an open mind to opportunity.

Because there is opportunity in and through creating content, another type of project that you can do provides a good way you can get published for free. For example, I have worked on some projects for professionals, such as for attorneys. It is called *Lone Star Business Leaders Houston | Edition - Volume 1.* Within it, there are 10 different attorneys with varying expertise—such as marketing, transition assistance, how to use the post 9/11 GI Bill, or any veteran business— so they do not walk all over each other. Each of them does a chapter. The format is that I interview them based on One Problem, One Solution. Their interview content becomes their chapter so they do not have to write anything. Everyone in the book benefits, including the person with the least expertise also gets their chapter done. The News is wrapped all around that too, so everyone gets to go on a ride. This type of book could even be put together for an entire group. Through the formulas we have successfully used, you can position yourself as an authority in such a way that increasingly compounds your celebrity as well as your business.

Benefits of Becoming Published

Although earlier in the book it mentions the various benefits of you yourself taking the authority journey, it is worth reiterating some of those benefits as specific to publishing.

In fact, there are multiple benefits that result from being a published author. You will see that if you are not published that you are missing out on opportunities right and left—some of which you may not have even realized before.

- **Your Instant Credibility**
  First of all—and most notably—having a published book gives you instant credibility as an expert.

Think about it from a customer's standpoint. If you need to hire a real estate agent to sell your home, Agent A gives you listing information along with a business card, but Agent B gives you listing information along with a published book.

Who would you choose to sell your home? Your initial impression would most likely be that Agent B is an authority. So, I bet you answered Agent B. Whatever industry you are in, you can have that type of weighted credibility.

- **Your Message Benefits Others**
  Your message is important. By publishing your message in a book and a variety of formats, such as in articles and blogs, it crystalizes your message

  As part of your authority positioning, the important information uniquely conveyed in your book becomes available to your market to benefit from the conciseness of your message as well as can grasp who you are and what you can do for them as potential clients.

  Nearly any professional can benefit from having a published book available—particularly when they have copies on hand to distribute for marketing purposes.

  Having a book serves to educate, and persuade existing clients, new clients, and potential clients. It is especially effective in answering common questions about your services.

So what better way is there to convey your message in an impactful way than to physically hand people your message in a published book?

- **You Increase Your Client Base and Your Sales**
  Giving your book to a client or potential client helps you to become the person who knows about your industry. Whether they read it and put it on their shelf or just put it directly on their shelf, the good news is they are advertising you and your business!
  Existing clients continue to view you as the best so they want to remain your client; and potential clients seek your services, which makes it easier to get prospects commit to doing business with you so that your sales increase.

- **You Charge More Money**
  As an author, you are considered to be an expert on your subject and can charge more money for your services.

- **You Receive a Residual Income**
  A best-selling book could be another stream of income for you while you are vacationing or while you are receiving a low commission.

Because there is a difference between getting Royalties and having Authority, it is important to explore the distinctions. People such as Stephen King and E. L. James make money by selling a lot of books, where they receive Royalties based on the book sales. As an entrepreneur or a business owner, however, you create expert status, credibility and authority because you wrote the book on your topic regarding how you do business. In both regards, you can have a best seller, although one may generate Royalties for a celebrity author such as King or James; and another best seller may not generate Royalties, but will create Authority.

- **You Get Invited to Speaking Events**
  By the mere fact that you are an author, people want to hear what you have to say. Even if no one has read your book, you are viewed as an authority and will attract more clients.

- **You Manage Your Reputation**
  When you have a book, you can proactively manage your business' reputation. A Google search will pull up your authorship page and sometimes your book's sales page above other searchable public information, such as divorce proceedings or the like.

- **You Receive Many More Benefits**
  Being published brings ongoing opportunities and benefits that cannot always be predicted.

Now that you know some of the many benefits you can expect as a published author, knowing the types of books to publish and how to get the book done in the first place are the next important steps.

To get your message to your target audience is more accessible in today's world of modern technology—particularly through self-publishing.

Publishing Power via Self-Publishing

While there are benefits to publishing with a major publisher and to self-publishing, the focus of this chapter is on self-publishing as it provides more access to a wider base of entrepreneurs who have a message to convey and can readily get it published.

Although the process of publishing a book can be fun and exciting, there are also roadblocks that often come up. Knowing how to navigate through the components of a self-published book is essential.

The great news is that you do not need to be a book publishing expert to release a high-quality book.

While you reap the benefits of having a published book, you can have a publishing professional take care of the content (based upon your ideas as provided in an interview), formatting, editing, cover creation and marketing details.

Writing a book is even easier than you think, especially once you really know how to do it. Depending upon the type of book that you want to write, there are techniques and approaches you can use to write a book very quickly—even quicker than seven days!

Unfortunately, most people go through their lives without knowing what it feels like to be a published author. It is quite an accomplishment—and is now easier more than ever!

There is still work involved, though, in knowing what to do and how. The good news is that my team and I specialize in every aspect of your publishing needs to make you a published author—and even a Best-Selling Author!

This news should be very exciting for you because most people do not have a published book, which allows you to set yourself apart from your competition, where quite possibly, you can be the only professional in your town with your own published book in digital and/or print formats.

Digital and Print Book Types

There are advantages to both digital and print books. With the demand for print and digital technology today, you can easily publish your book in both forms. One of the great benefits of having a digital book format is that it allows you to extend your reach. However, you will also want a physical book available for people in your local area as well as for people with whom you connect.

In this part, I will give you the core information regarding the fastest and easiest ways to publish both a digital and a print version of your book.

Benefits of Digital Publishing

Digital Self-Publishing has been growing exponentially with even more potential on the horizon.

In particular, Amazon's Kindle market is huge! There are millions of Kindle owners worldwide downloading and reading Kindle books. And the market is expanding even more ever since the release of Kindle into retail stores, such as Wal-Mart, Target, Best Buy and Staples.

What is even more amazing about being a Kindle Publisher is that Kindle readers do not even need to own a Kindle to read Kindle books because anyone with a PC, Mac, iPad, iPod, iPhone or Android device can download any of the Kindle Apps so they can immediately purchase and read Kindle books.

This fact alone provides instant access to your content to even more millions of potential customers. By publishing your work through Kindle, you can earn anywhere from 35% to 70% on your book sales. You can publish any type of your content through Kindle: Short stories; Novels; Recipe books; How-to guides; and so on. The list is endless. Imagine the possibilities of how much additional income from your published work as well as opportunities to leverage your expertise that Kindle provides.

Kindle, however, is not the only self-publisher on the web. There are various other self-publishers (such as Smashwords), which can make your book available to important booksellers like Barnes & Noble. Having this variety further expands your potential market.

Benefits of Print Publishing

Although eBooks (aka, digital books) are easier to distribute and do not require physical space, eBooks cannot replicate every element and advantage of books in print.

If you are a local expert or are an expert in any niche, having print books can expand your personal brand more substantially than digital books. Because a print book is a physical object with tangible qualities, it is something real that you can touch and see versus an eBook in digital form that has no weight and does not take up space. When you give someone a print book, they can see it, which increases the likelihood that they will read it.

A major *perceived* difference between print books and eBooks is that eBooks can be made by anyone.
Any type of writer—from the worst to the best—can publish an eBook.

However, with today's print-on-demand technology, the same is true because it allows you to print a book without going through publishers and editors. Most people do not realize that it is now easier to self-publish.

With your book in a print format, it demonstrates how you are serious about your expertise as well as that you have gone through the publishing process to make your information available.

Print books are a perfect way to demonstrate your expertise and gain credibility. Moreover, people tend to comprehend information and retain more details from printed materials, which provide you with opportunity to show your knowledge and experience.

Benefits of Publishing in Both Formats

You can even mix by cross-referencing them. For example, you can provide digital marketing content directly within your print book by adding a website, a social media page, or a QR code to bring people to your online space.

It is possible to mix physical advertising with your digital presence, although it is much more difficult because you have to ship those physical books and/or other materials such as brochures to potential clients. During the time that it takes to ship those items, your potential client might have already chosen another company.

The best of both worlds is when you provide your book in both formats—in digital and in print so people can chose which format they prefer. By leveraging your expertise as a published author, you reinforce your authority that provides you with additional marketing, speaking and even publishing opportunities that open up as you move further along your authority journey.

Chapter 15 - Speaking as The Authority

Another one of the most important components in establishing your authority platform on a widespread basis is to become a speaker who speaks in a variety of venues.

These are two basic parts of the speaking equation:

(1) Creating a signature speech based on your journey and core message, which can be modified as needed.
(2) Having an audience that you reach either from your own platform or from someone else's platform.

When you add the goal of increasing your influence and sales, you add the third part of how important it is to market subtly, yet effectively the products and/or services you provide [including your book(s)] by the value you provide within the message you are delivering.

Because publishing, speaking and marketing are distinct, yet integrally connect, it is important to have this chapter focus solely on how essential speaking as the authority is to your increased business success.

Benefits of Becoming a Speaker
Various components within The Authority Code Formula involve speaking in an array of venues, including the Authority Interview; News Releases related to your speaking opportunities; Best-Seller Campaigns that often include aspects of speaking; Internet Radio Shows that may be your own and/or other people's; Video Interviews; and Speaking opportunities themselves.

By speaking as the authority in these and other venues, it is a powerful way for you to share your expertise as you connect with and communicate directly with those in your market who can benefit from your message as well as increase your business, which can be mutually beneficial to you and to those you serve.

In turn, many of those people spread your message and refer to you as an authority, which is that third-party endorsement that can be even more valuable to positioning you as an authority.

The benefits of becoming a speaker are closely linked with the other authority-building results mentioned early on within this book as well as are specifically related to each form of speaking venue as you (the speaker) and the speaking venue itself merge in a combined focus of reaching the target audience.

It is important to note that although many people fear public speaking, if you view it as an opportunity to share your expertise and focus on the people you can help rather than on your fears and concerns, you can overcome that fear and learn to enjoy the opportunity and benefits that go along with speaking.

As you speak the first time, it gets easier. Even highly experienced people indicate that they still have fear, but move through it by preparing and going out there to speak anyway.

There are also some speaking organizations that you can join, which allow you to continue to sharpen your skills as a speaker as well as to connect you with others who speak on different topics. I joined The Public Speakers Association; and intentionally accepted the role of being a Director in order to take on leadership as a speaker.

When I am connecting with my target market, I can refer to my positioning as a leader within the speaking profession, which adds to my credibility. When you are creating and maintaining your authority position, it requires you to take on leadership in various ways as well as to humbly let others know so that they are aware of your authority position.

Speaking is powerful because it makes your message come alive as well as adds more depth to your authority because the assumption of you being on the platform is that you have a message worth delivering—and the great news is that you do when you package it appropriately.

By communicating your message in a variety of venues, it provides you with an opportunity to spread your message to many other people in a way that provides information conveyed through your voice tone and/or facial expressions that emphasize the power of what you say.

- **You gain instant credibility**
  Speaking from the various platforms, such as via Internet Radio, CDs, Stages, and so forth differentiates you in eyes of consumer because it automatically places you in a position of instant credibility, similar to how being published does.

- **You make a difference by your message**
  When you speak, you make a difference as you communicate your message through the power of the spoken word that brings it alive and gets it out to the market as well as reinforces the impact you as a published author make—although speakers can and do make a difference even if they have not yet published a book. However, both are highly recommended in building your authority.

- **You increase your client base**
  As you speak in person, on internet radio and/or through CDs, you have the opportunity to increase your potential clients as well as to demonstrate to your existing clients that you are still the sought-after expert.

  The various components of creating and maintaining your authority status—especially through speaking opportunities—afford you the ability to grow your client base, where you increasingly become hunted as people seek you to work with, although you do still need to stay open and ready to seek opportunity as well.

- **You increase your sales**
  With more of a client base, it provides more opportunity to increase your sales. When you speak, it is key to always have an offer that you provide—the more irresistible, the better. However, you need to be sure that what you do provide does deliver on the value to your client so they benefit from it as well as become a long-term one.

- **You charge more money**
  By being an expert, you can charge more for your speaking fees as well as have more people in your audience so that more people are in attendance where you can make a difference as well as where have more potential sales, which boosts potential income for your expertise.

- **You get invited to join other events/projects**

Because you are out there on the speaking circuit, when people hear your message that provides value, it attracts more opportunity to speak at other events and be a part of other projects. Again, you can shift the direction of the tide so you become hunted by others desiring your expertise.

- **You manage your reputation**
  As you are actively engaging your audiences and making a difference for them, you become real and they witness your genuine desire to make a difference. By sending out News Releases related to your speaking opportunities, you call attention to being out there engaged with your market—and may even attract more positive News.

- **You receive many more benefits**
  Your speaking opportunities themselves provide compounding effects that when coupled with publishing ones and even tripled with other marketing venues, many more benefits arise for you that can also benefit how you serve your clients.

Speaking Power via Multiple Venues

Although many of the benefits derived from speaking overall have already been touched upon within this chapter, it is worthwhile to distinguish a few more benefits as related to a few key distinctions between speaking formats.

By speaking in one venue, you can take your message to another venue. So that it is not always the same, it is good to make it relevant to your audience as well as to the times—although some content may be consistently relevant because it is principle-based.

Over time, you will create a speaking (and authority) presence that exists across platforms and over time. Such platforms can range from pre-recorded audios and/or videos to live or pre-recorded radio interviews as well as to live events, which themselves may be recorded.

These and other variations provide you with opportunity to spread your message to many people simultaneously or at different times and across times when they listen again, if it was previously recorded.

By breaking each opportunity type down further, we can identify some additional benefits of these three main facets of being either pre-recorded or live as well as the third option of being live while being recorded to be used in the future as pre-recorded.

Benefits of Pre-recorded Speaking

Some of the great things about speaking when it is pre-recorded is that you as the speaker get to have it edited so that if there is something that occurs, such as coughing or mispronunciation of a word, that it can be deleted or corrected.

Often times, when there are pros, there are cons. So, the con side of pre-recorded speaking is that it needs to be well edited so that the way it is edited does not lose your original intent and emphasis. When possible, if you can have say in the editing process as well as the final product, it would be ideal.

Another major benefit is that a pre-recorded speaking opportunity does not come with some of the other challenges that accompany a live presentation. However, it is still essential to prepare for the specific format so that you are at your best.

Benefits of Live Speaking

Excitement is in the air at a live speaking event—that is, if you help bring that excitement. A live event provides interaction with the audience and other speakers who are there and are enthusiastic about the theme and industry.

With a live event, your audience may be excited about who you are and what you do, although you may or may not have product and/or services they can buy so they can continue to benefit from the value you offer. So, be sure to be ready with something to offer beyond the live event so you maximize the opportunity for yourself and your audience of potential clients. If you do not have a product to offer you are doing a disservice to your audience.

Benefits of Recording Live Events

The best of both worlds is having a live event as well as having some or all of it recorded because you get to experience the hype of the event as well as have the recording to get transcribed for written content and edited for audio/video content.

One important factor to keep in mind, though, that if you are recording someone else besides just yourself that you get written permission and/or have it be part of your event participation agreement that by their presence they are agreeing to being recorded by audio and/or video as part of the audience. As you can see, getting quality legal advice from the right attorney for various aspects of your business is vital.

Whether it is a pre-recorded venue, live venue or a combination of both in some way, you leverage your expertise as a speaker as you reinforce your authority that provides you with additional marketing, publishing and even speaking opportunities that open up as you continue simultaneously reinforcing your authority on your journey.

To Schedule a No Obligation Authority Breakthrough Session
To learn more about "The Authority Mindset"
Additional video training is available at
www.theincomparibleauthority.com
or www.claimyourauthoritynow.com

Chapter 16 – Marketing as The Authority

Using *The Authority Code* approach leverages who you are and what you can do. The key is to continue to market yourself as you reinforce your credibility and authority to generate more traffic leads and then turn a high percentage of the leads into closed sales.

These are the two basic parts of the marketing equation:

(1) Identifying your market.
(2) Marketing to your market.

Knowing your market and marketing consistently to them sounds simple. However, the market changes and marketing approaches continually change. There are certain principles and practices that remain consistent, including the basic principles underlying The Authority Code that include the various components of leveraging your authority.

Because publishing, speaking and marketing are distinct, yet integrally connect, it is important to have a chapter on each of them, where this chapter focuses solely on how marketing as the authority is to your increased business success.

Three Marketing Methods
Once you know your market, keep the following three methods in mind as you strategically leverage your expert status:

> *Method One* – Selling More of Your Products and/or Services to Existing Clients
>
> *Method Two* – Separating Yourself Apart from Competition to Attract New Clients

Method Three – Updating Your Existing Marketing

Let me explain more about what I mean. First of all, it is worthy to mention that although these are three "methods," they are all actually the outcomes of one overarching and united method of becoming an authority that enables you to achieve the results that these three "methods" target. However, it is still useful to identify them as separate, yet related methods.

Method One is about retaining your current client base so you can continue to provide value for them and sell more of your products and/or services to them. Using a little "humble brag" gets the word out so your client base knows about each media appearance or book deal or book launch hitting a Best Seller List, and so forth. To systematically get the word out, you can use an email campaign and/or social media posts. We can work with you on exactly what to say.

A brief example of a humble brag could be something such as: "I have exciting news! *The Wall Street Journal* just ran an interview I did about the new method I have to help many Americans become millionaires." Another example of a humble brag could be connected to what is known as a "news jack." Someone did this type of humble brag in response to the fastest growing number of millionaires being in Asia Pacific. For this type of approach, first, you share something on social media; then tie it to a related current topic or story that is already in the media; and then when the media picks up your comments, you do a humble brag to your client base.

In regard to your book, in particular, it is especially important to mention that you were picked up by the various media sites for becoming a Best-selling Author. The media reinforces that you are a newsworthy authority—and that further communicates your value without you having to be the one directly stating it yourself.

On the other hand, *Method Two* separates you from competition in such a way that it more easily attracts new clients because new prospects have far less resistance because they recognize you as a celebrity and as an authority.

Being a published author naturally sets you apart because there may be hundreds (if not thousands) of qualified experts in your industry within your target market. However, not many (and possibly very few) are authors about their expertise. So, when new prospects are looking for who to do business with in your industry, for instance, you would stand out—especially if you have an online presence that shows your book(s) and media coverage.

To paraphrase Dan Kennedy, one of the greatest marketers, he says *"that the simple truth is if you are not deliberate in systematically, methodically or rapidly and dramatically establishing yourself as an authority, at least to your clientele and target market, you are asleep at the wheel, ignoring what is fueling the entire economy around you, neglecting development of a measurable, valuable asset."*

For example, if you are a real estate agent, homeowners and motivated sellers have a better chance of picking you because you are a published author—and beyond that, you are a Best-selling Author. This status has a compounding effect because it also makes it easy for others to refer you and to recommend you to their friends.*(In fact, I could write a book on just how many opportunities have opened up for me after having written a book and having become a Best-selling Author. It has been incredible!)*

You get referrals because people pass on your name and talk about your authority. Other people look at you differently from before—including your friends and family. It becomes easier to get one more deal each month because of being that authority, that author, that Best-selling Author. It is so powerful that it is worth repeating in various ways throughout this book so you see for yourself how you can use The Authority Code to make these breakthroughs happen for you.

Lots of amazing opportunities upon opportunities open up when you are an author and authority!

Another one of my favorite examples happened while I was in a waiting room one morning and a gentleman struck up a conversation with me. I happened to be wearing a Pebble Beach Golf shirt. Our interaction went something like the following:

> He commented, "That's a pretty tough course. Have you played it?"
>
> I looked up and replied, "No, I haven't; but I like the shirt and the course." I then continue to answer emails and respond to clients on my tablet.
>
> He persists on starting a conversation by asking, "Do you train or coach people? By your presence and the way you carry yourself, I would listen to what you have to say."
>
> I stopped and looked up again as I said, "As a matter of fact I do! I help people claim their authority in their market. I am a speaker and International Best-selling Author!"

His whole demeanor changed. He affirmed, "I thought you were somebody like that." He continues on to say, "The only thing I have done is that I have a Patent!"

Now he had my attention. For months, I had been looking for a solution to impact the world and help Veterans with jobs to get them off the street. My vision had been inspired by a young lady in Detroit who made coats for homeless people and gave them jobs to make them—and I wanted to create an opportunity like that to make a difference.

He told me what he had the patent on, but said that he did not know the next steps that he needed to take.

I give him my two recent Best-selling books: *BOLD!* and *The Authority Mindset*. He asked me, "What do I owe you for these?"

I said, "They are a gift!"

It turns out that his patent is in a $2 Billion Dollar niche that currently has a 40% waste! It would save Millions (if not Billions) globally. I got the meeting scheduled—and he now knows the next steps that will lead to the next steps. That is what I do: I help people like him get the attention needed to make things happen.

Method 3 is to update your existing marketing. Once you add to your email signature or your auto-responder, you can add your newfound authority of being a "Best-selling Author" at the bottom. Use trust triggers (such as "As seen on ABC, CBS, NBC, Fox and CNN") on websites, social media properties, email footer, business cards, video intros, and even your book(s). Put it everywhere!

What I teach is called The Authority Code. By its very nature, it is cyclical and is designed to keep you in the media. We can start anywhere here in the formula. Here is a list of the types of media-related activities the formula includes, which are listed in the general order in which we do for our clients:

- Do Your *The Best-selling Author Campaign*
- Hold Your *Authority Interview (that is a published interview that can be done without you writing a word since we do the interview, get it transcribed, and get it smoothed out by our writer.*
- Write and Distribute Your *Article* (that gets syndicated and picked up by the media)
- Position Yourself as a *Major Network Media Contributor* (who contributes either monthly or weekly)
- Set Up Your *Podcast* (to get your audio out there on iTunes where people can download your information as an educator and advocate teaching and educating them about what you do)
- Generate Various *Spin-Off Articles* from your Original Article (including changing from first person to third person, or vice versa)
    - Some examples may include: Spotlight Article, News Jacking-style Article
- Publish Your Expertise in another *Kindle Book with your Article*
- Create *News Releases* using Various Types of Content
- Provide *Free Reports* for your target audience

The benefit is you are creating your own "Kardashian Effect" so that you generate more content, get more media coverage, get more authority, and get more business.

Staying in the news is a key part of The Authority Code!

Benefits of Marketing

The benefits of marketing are mentioned all throughout this book because the basis for The Authority Code as a book and The Authority Code Formula that it describes is all about marketing in the various forms while getting your message out to your market. To do more than provide a high-level outline of the benefits further here would be too redundant. Instead, it is important to just call your attention to the fact that there are many benefits to creating and maintaining your authority through marketing-type activities, which include the following that are mentioned in more detail elsewhere (including in the chapter on publishing):

- Your Instant Credibility
- Your Message Benefits Others
- You Increase Your Sales
- You Charge More Money
- You Receive a Residual Income
- You Get Invited to Speaking Events
- You Manage Your Reputation
- You Receive Many More Benefits

By leveraging your expertise through marketing, you reinforce your authority that provides you with additional opportunities through speaking, publishing, and marketing that open up as you move further along your authority journey.

To Schedule a No Obligation Authority Breakthrough Session
To learn more about "The Authority Mindset"
Additional video training is available at
www.theincomparibleauthority.com
or www.claimyourauthoritynow.com

Part IV

Applying The Exact Authority Code for Success

Your Authority Journey

Now that you have a grasp of what is involved in taking the authority journey to become the sought-after authority leader in your market, it is time for you to begin applying the exact formula to get the authority code actions compounding for you. It all starts with deciding that now is the time to claim your authority—and then taking formulaic actions to make it happen. By the end of the initial start-up phase of your journey, you will still be the amazing expert that you have been—although more and more people will know about who you are and what your expertise provides. Your leads, sales and profits should also continue to increase as you and your market become even more awakened to your authority as you increasingly introduce yourself as the authority within your market...

Chapter 17 - Timing Your Authority

It is true that it takes time to develop expertise in an area. However, many people are well equipped to claim their authority sooner than they think. Often times, people get stuck in learning more and more or proving themselves over and over before they know without a doubt that they are ready.

The problem is that perhaps their opportunity has passed them by when they finally muster the courage to do it.

The good news is that you get to choose to the timing of when you will actually claim your authority. Once you decide to do it, it could take you anywhere from the span of three months to three years (or more)—depending upon your choices and actions.

If you wait for recognition that may never even come, it will most likely be the longer timeframe. If, however, you take control and claim your authority by systematically creating it, it may be just a matter of months.

You may be asking yourself: "What is one of the most important actions I can take to claim my authority starting now?"

My recommendation—and one that I know works because I have done it and so have so many entrepreneurs—is not only for you to apply The Authority Code Formula as described throughout this book, but also for you to invest in a mentor who knows how to show you the way to claiming your authority.

As described elsewhere, the first round of applying the formula is your Start-up Phase to lay the groundwork to build upon. This first phase should be completed within a few months, if not sooner. Next is the Maintenance Phase occurs on a monthly basis, where you will repeatedly take the same type of action steps with some variation.

There are many benefits to having a top-quality mentor who has already achieved what you want to achieve so they have persevered through the many challenges that resulted in their success. The mentor help you see where to navigate through challenges so you can minimize (potentially avoid) the pain and frustration of trying to figure everything out because the mentor has already been down that path and found the way to the success you want.

Some of the most successful people in the world—whether they are in sports and/or in business—have or have had mentors. People like Tiger Woods, Payton Manning, Monica Seles, and Michael Jordan have all had mentors and coaches. For you to get to the next level, you also have to have a coach and a mentor.

I have invested in various mentors at various times in my career—and the payoffs keep coming! Due to the compounding positive effects of these various mentors as well as my willingness to be coachable and take action, I have a unique set of experience and skills that position me well to be a mentor to others who are ready to claim their authority.

There is a lot of work involved in providing mentorship. However, it is well worth it to see people finally being able to realize their dreams!

As you can see throughout the book, The Authority Code works. To streamline the process, I coach and guide people based on what I have already figured out works consistently for people to quickly claim their authority—and it can even happen for you!

For those of you who have a core message to share with your market and with the world and are interested to claim your Authority in a streamlined manner, my team and I can help you.

However, prior to working together to customize and implement The Authority Code Formula with you, you first need to meet the following criteria:

(1) Integrity
(2) Commitment
(3) Focus
(4) Dedication to meet target goals
(5) Desire to educate/advocate for your customers/clients
(6) Business that is legitimate
(7) Story to tell
(8) Expertise/value to deliver to the market and/or world
(9) Ability to invest in a mentor
(10) Perseverance to follow through on the coaching

This combined criterion is a very important part of your success. Being proactive about mentoring someone in their business to claim their authority takes real commitment on both the mentor's part and on the part of the person being mentored.

The timing of not only when, but how you claim your authority is important because the how part can impact how well it goes during the initial phase and ongoing phases as you cycle through The Authority Code Formula—so that one by one, minute by minute, day by day, week by week, month by month, year by year, and so on and so on... so that your authority legacy compounds with every client you serve and every product you create.

Now is the time to take action to claim your authority!

Chapter 18 – Customizing Your Authority Code

While you discovered the essential keys to creating your authority that is available to you through The Authority Code Formula as described in Chapter 12, this chapter provides a high-level, yet important outline that corresponds with the formula content in order to provide a customization framework designed to provide you with a basis for applying the formula to your authority-building strategy.

The first part of this chapter focuses on the Start-up Phase, which is the first round of going through the steps of the formula. The latter part of the chapter focuses on the Maintenance Phase, which can include going through the entire formula again, yet must at least include the "condensed version" of some of the key codes that you need to repeat consistently over time. Chapter 13 emphasized these two primary phases as being an important part of laying the foundation for your authority and then reinforcing it.

Because there is so much involved in implementing each of these—specifically related to how to customize them individually—this book aims to provide you with the streamlined highlights of what is entailed in claiming your authority.

As previously mentioned, the reason I am able to provide this streamlined formula is because my authority journey has led me to become The Authority Syndicate who supports people in claiming their authority faster as well as setting them on a path of sustained authority.

Since the reality is I only have so much time, I can only work with a select number of clients at a given time. That is why I also created an Online Course called "The Authority Academy" that is available at www.AuthorityOnFire.com and provides even more guidance regarding how to customize your authority journey so that it provides even more detailed support for those who want to do their own self-paced journey.

It is important to note that this book, *The Authority Code,* streamlines the process in a formulaic way, which is groundbreaking because it is the first time it is presented in this manner. The Online Course provides significant information that is not included within this book. Although it is closely related to the contents of this book, it is not necessarily arranged to systematically align with this book as it is in and of itself a separate product with its own distinct value.

I highly recommend that you refer to both this book and the course while using this customization chapter as a way to consolidate notes you have from both of the sources about each type of authority-building code as you build your authority step by step.

For easy reference, I have provided The Authority Code Formula below. However, feel free to refer back to Chapter 12 for additional information about each code component as the remainder of this chapter is focused on applying and tracking your steps. Throughout this chapter, there are periodic reminders for you to reflect on what other actions to take. Although it may be highly repetitious for one chapter to have so many reminders, it is intentional so you have opportunity to pause and plan as you tailor the formula application to your specific authority-building process.

Your Authority Code Customization - Planning & Tracking

Within this section about tracking the Initial Start-Up Phase, each component is listed according to the order in which it is listed in the formula. There is a small chart at the beginning of this section where you can insert the date you will be completing each step. Also, there is individualized information about each component that you can fill in before, during, and/or after you actually take the actions. It is best to quickly glance through this entire section so you can see what is recommended as part of your tracking. However, feel free to add other aspects as well, although you want to keep it at a high enough level that the details do not prevent you from taking action. If you work with an authority-building expert, it reduces the learning curve and maximizes the benefit you receive.

The planning and tracking of each code is key so that you are clear about what action(s) you are taking related to each one as well as to where you are in the process. The codes represent the high-level actions and results related to each main step listed within the formula.

The Authority Code Formula
AI + 2AA + 3PR + BSC + IR + CON + DM + OC + IMR + VI + SP = Authority Positioning Established

As mentioned elsewhere, each code may involve various sub-codes and/or actions involved in order to produce the high-level result.

The small chart below is where you can *insert the dates* in the blank space above each code components so it indicates when you will be completing the step for each code. It is important to keep in mind, however, that there is usually a process involved in completing each one so you can allow enough time for each one.

AI	AA	AA	PR	PR	BSC	IR	CON	DM	OC	VI	SP	IMR

Throughout this chapter, there is also individualized information about each component that you can fill in before, during, and/or after you actually take the actions. It is best to quickly glance through this entire section so you can see what is recommended as part of your tracking. However, feel free to add other aspects as well, although you want to keep it at a high enough level that the details do not prevent you from taking action.

Before Applying The Authority Code Formula Action Steps...
In addition to ensuring that you have a website, it is important to get set up to track your leads, sales and profits by measuring your baseline, current, and target results for increased success. Some of it involves daily tracking while others involves monthly or annual tracking, which are both measured on the daily results that add up day after day, week after week, and month after month. As you go through your authority journey the first time and then take the monthly authority-reinforcement/expansion actions as shown in the condense formula, you may find your results are lower or higher than your target goals, which you can adjust accordingly so you are increasing the bar while keeping it within reach.

Measuring Leads
Current Number of Business
Leads____
Target Number of Business
Leads____

Actual Number of Business Leads____

Change between Current Baseline Number and Actual Number (in percentage)

____

Difference between Target Number and Actual Number (in percentage) ______________________________________

Measuring Sales

Current Number of Overall Sales (Year-To-Date)

____

Average Number of Monthly Sales (Based on Prior Year)

____

Current Number of Product Sales by Product (Year-To-Date)

____

Average Number of Service Sales by Service (Year-To-Date)

____

Target Number of Overall Sales____

Actual Number of Overall Sales____

Change between Current Number of Overall Sales and Actual Number (in percentage) _____________________________

Difference between Target Number and Actual Number (in percentage) ______________________________________

Measuring Profits

Current Income (Year-To-Date)

____

Profit & Loss (Year-To-Date)

____

Profit & Loss (Based on Prior Year)

____

Average Monthly Income (Based on Prior Year)

____

Target Monthly Income____

Actual Monthly
Income____
Change between Current Income and Actual Income (in percentage) ____________________________________
Difference between Target Income and Actual Income (in percentage) ____________________________________

Identifying My Authority-Building Milestones & Micro-Specialization

It is important to begin with the end result of your Authority Positioning that you are aiming to achieve so that you have a vision for yourself and your business regarding how you will serve others through your products and/or services.

So, instead of ending with Authority Positioning at the bottom of this chapter, you first need to identify the milestones of you Authority Journey that lead you to where you are now; and then pinpoint your Micro-Specialization related to your desired Authority Positioning as well as the related Products and/or Services to your business vision.

The positioning that you seek does not have to be tied to your past journey, but chances are that along the way there were experiences that are connected in some way or another. Even if there was a major leap in a new direction, identifying that will help you see when you started developing and/or recognizing your strengths and passion for the positioning you seek.

A good starting point is to reflect in a journal, which does not need to be a fancy journal. The important thing is that you reflect. You may be wondering what to reflect about since you do not know what you want yet. Start by writing down what you think and feel. Reflect back about where you have come in your life and career journey so far. It may help if you write to a younger version and/or older version of yourself and tell yourself what you should do. Perhaps it will give you some insights and perspectives that nudge you to take action in the direction you want to go, yet cannot quite see right now. My recommendation is that in addition to journaling that you read self-improvement books to get your mind and thoughts on track with what it takes to be an entrepreneur. You may even want to create a Reading List—and start one book at a time. As you have your thoughts begin to crystallize, you will be able to answer the following types of questions in a more fulfilling manner so that it truly does become what you desire.

- Milestones of My Authority Journey [up to now]

____
____
____
____
____

- Pinpoint Description of My Micro-Specialized Authority Positioning

____
____
____
____
____

- Products and/or Services [including description and pricing] related to My Business Vision

____
____
____
____
____

- My Sales Funnel [progression of product and service upsell and downsell offerings]

____
____
____
____
____

Now that you have a big picture of the journey that lead you where you are now as well as your vision for your Authority Positioning and related products and/or services, you are ready to begin applying the formula.

Applying The Authority Code Formula for The START-UP PHASE [Planning & Tracking]

Authority Interview

- Date of Interview

  ____
  ____
  ____

- Interviewer

  ____
  ____
  ____

- Radio Platform

  ____
  ____
  ____

- My Authority Topic (One Problem One Solution)____

  ____
  ____

- Identify Key Milestones of My Journey [Note: Refer above to the appropriate section(s)]

  ____

- Create Checklist of My Preparation Tasks prior to Interview
- Provide Recommended Q&As w/ bullet-pointed answers
- Create Follow-up Checklist of After-Interview Tasks

- Save the Link to the Interview on my computer; post the Link in my website's Media Room; and write the Link's domain name

- Consider other aspects to track using a checklist

1st – AA = Authority Association

- Title of Article creating Authority Association – to be published in *Business Innovators Magazine* (BIM) [interview-style format]

- Date Article to be published
- List reasons being associated with their top experts/celebrities provides authority positioning
- Get document with "Authority Interview" transcription as basis for article
- Complete Short Questionnaire to provide info for article
- Create Checklist for My Preparation for BIM article
- Proofread article (if available option)
- Approve after final changes (if available option)
- Save the LINK to my BIM article on my computer and post in my website's Media Room

____

____

____

- Get both a hard copy and a digital copy of the BIM in which my article was published:

  ____

  ____

  ____

- Consider other aspects to track using a Checklist

  ____

  ____

  ____

  ____

  ____

2nd – AA = Authority Association

- Title of Article creating Authority Association – to be published in *Small Business Trendsetters* [feature-style format]

  ____

  ____

  ____

- Date Article to be published________________________________

  ____

  ____

- Get document with "Authority Interview" transcription as basis for article

  ____

  ____

  ____

- Complete Short Questionnaire to provide info for article

  ____

____

____

- Create Checklist for My Preparation for SBT article

  ____

  ____

  ____

  ____

  ____

- Proofread article (if available option)

  ____

  ____

- Approve after final changes (if available option)

  ____

  ____

- Save the LINK to my SBT article on my computer and post in my website's Media Room

  ____

  ____

  ____

- Get a hard copy and digital copy of the SBT in which my article was published:

  ____

  ____

  ____

- Consider other aspects to track using a Checklist

  ____

  ____

  ____

  ____

3PR = 3 News Releases

It is important to be actively creating and reinforcing your authority while also keeping The News informed. In general, after each significant formula code-based activity you perform as you follow the Authority Formula, create and distribute a News

Release (NR). The three most important ones to get your authority launched are for you to release News Releases for your Authority Interview, your BIM article, and your SBT article (as listed below). You can create a News Release template as well as leverage similar content to use for various News Releases.

- News Release #1 – Immediately following the release of your Authority Interview [create NR and distribute]
- News Release #2 – Immediately following the publication of your Business Innovators Magazine article [create NR and distribute]
- News Release #3 – immediately following the publication of your Small Business Trends article [create NR and distribute]
- News Release #4 – immediately following each important activity you take in building your authority [create NR and distribute]

For each News Release, consider which aspects you need to follow up and follow through on. It may be beneficial to create a running log of News Releases using a simple tracking document that includes the following types of categories:

Date Submitted	NR Document Name	What NR promotes	Where submitted	Post NR in Media Room	Results

BSC = Published "Best Seller Campaign"

An important part of this code component of having a Best Seller Campaign is that you have a book written in the first place. Many people find it challenging to know how to get their book written so there is one to promote. My team and I have streamlined the process to work with clients so they get their book developed without even having to write a word—yet, it is their book because they provided their ideas during the interview format.

Book Development Phase –

- Identify your book topic related to your expertise____

  ____
- Identify the primary topics that will form the Table of Contents

  ____

  ____

  ____

  ____

  ____
- Date of Interview to be used for Book One Problem on Soulution____

  ____
- Name of Interviewer____

  ____

  ____
- Document File Name of Transcribed Interview____

  ____
- Milestones with Target Dates of Book Development Process

  ____

  ____

  ____

  ____

  ____

Publishing Phase –

- Publication Date__________
- Publisher__________
- Publishing Process Setup (including contract agreements)
- Publishing Process Actions
- Publishing Process Follow-up Actions

Marketing Phase –

- Best Seller Campaign Plan – [Before Phase: Actions to Take and When, including Managing Leads, Sales and Profits]

____

____

- Best Seller Campaign Plan – [During Phase: Implement Plan and Check off Actions as Complete Each One]

  ____

  ____

  ____

  ____

  ____

- Best Seller Campaign Plan – [After Phase: Implement Plan and Leverage Your Best-selling Author Status]
- ____

  ____

  ____

  ____

  ____

- Post Link in Media Room for Published Book

  ____

  ____

- Post Link in Media Room for News Release______________________________________

  ____

- Post Link in Media Room for Other Key Aspects of Campaign [such as Links to Articles, etc.)____

IR = Internet Radio
The actions required may differ if it is your own Internet Radio Show or if it is someone else's that you are a Guest on. Either way, you want to get the audio recording as well as the transcribed content for it so you can leverage it in various ways, such as being book content, article content, etc. by changing the

medium in which the content gets distributed. It starts, however, by having you be on the Internet Radio. Create a running log of Internet Radio Shows you have been on as well as other ones you want to be on. If you have an Internet Radio Show, create a log of who you have had on the show as well as who you may want to have on your show. Below is a list of items to consider for one or both scenarios, where it may be your program or another person's program.

Date of Internet Radio
Show____

____

Identify Topic for the Radio Show as well as related Key Points

____

____

____

____

____

Follow up with Host regarding specifics required for being prepared for the Content for the Internet Radio Show

____

____

____

If you are the Host, create Checklists regarding what to do **Before the Internet Radio Show** related to:

- Producing The Show

  ____

  ____

  ____

  ____

  ____

  ____

- Content for The Show

  ____
  ____
  ____
  ____
  ____
  ____

During the Internet Radio Show, follow the appropriate Checklists to ensure it goes smoothly

____
____
____
____
____

After the Internet Radio Show:

- Post the Link within your website's Media Room______________________________________
  ____
  ____

- Get the Transcription and Leverage the Content in Various Other Formats____________________________________

[Repeat the process, as needed]

Running Log of Internet Radio Shows I have been a Guest on:

____
____
____
____
____

Running Log of Internet Radio Shows I want to be a Guest on (either for the first time or as a repeat):

____
____
____
____
____

If you have your own program, create a Running Log for:

- Topics for Internet Radio Shows

  ____
  ____
  ____
  ____
  ____
  _

- Guests for Internet Radio Shows

  ____
  ____
  ____
  ____
  ____
  _

CON = Content

Since the Content section within Chapter 12 is involves a lot of information, refer to that section as you reflect upon your core message(s) as well as how you can best communicate using various formats across various distribution venues.

My Micro-specialized Core Message(s)

____
____
____

____
____
____
____

Frequency of Updating	Content Distribution Type	Content Format(s)
Quarterly	LinkedIn	Profile
Monthly	LinkedIn	Article
Ongoing [per Media Attn.]	Website Page	Media Room Links

DM = Digital Magazine

In considering the Digital Magazine venues, you may choose to have your own digital magazine and/or have articles within someone else's digital magazine. If you want to pursue one or both, it is important to outline your actions so you can track them. This section would be similar to what would be involved with the Internet Radio actions, although the medium is in print rather than being auditory. Refer to the Internet Radio section for ideas in addition to those mentioned within this section.

- For publishing your own article in someone else's digital magazine, make a list of which ones you want to reach out to for consideration.

  ____
  ____
  ____
  ____
  ____
  ____
  ____
  ____

- For creating your own digital magazine, consider the title of it as well as the branding and cover. You may also want to list out potential contributors to your magazine as well as how often you want to publish it.

- Title

  ____

  ____

  ____

- Brand / Theme

  ____

  ____

  ____

- Cover Design

  ____

  ____

  ____

- News Releases about your various articles can reinforce your authority even more. So also refer to that section as well.

  ____

  ____

  ____

OC = Online Course

For the online course, you may want to consider referring to the book developing, publishing and marketing section to modify it for creating the online course. There will be differences, yet there are enough similarities that it is worth referring to as you customize your actions for this section. You may also find some other good ideas within Chapter 18 that would apply to this section.

Some key aspects of the Online Course are that you need to know the purpose and outcome results upfront so you are aware of what you are teaching. Since you are an expert in your micro-niche, be sure to focus on what your market needs to know so they are fully informed of what is important for them to know as your client base.

To create your online course, consider the following high-level steps in addition to others you may add, delete, or modify:

- Determine the name of your Online Course

  ____

  ____

- Outline your Online Course so that each part of your outline becomes a Training Module itself

  ____

  ____

  ____

  ____

  ____

  ____

  ____

  ____

- Determine the names of each Training Module for consistency with the overall Online Course as well as describe the module's contents

  ____

  ____

  ____

  ____

  ____

  ____

  ____

  ____

- Create an outline for each of the Training Modules, which will become the baseline for your Videos and PDFs (where each module has both)

- Make a checklist of items to do to create your Videos for the Online Course

- Make a checklist of items to do to create your PDFs for the Online Course

- Create a Marketing Message that describes the features and benefits of your Online Course

- Use your Marketing Message in your product description and/or on your website that describes your Online Course

- Create a Video [with a Script] for Marketing your Online Course

- Set up an eCommerce avenue to collect online payments that also digitally delivers the Online Course

VI = Video Interview

Video is a powerful way to both convey your message as well as connect with your audience. In addition to some of the high level actions listed below, be sure to refer to any other code component actions that may be helpful here.

- Create Video Interview with key talking points you want to cover in your message
- Research best practices for video interviews so you are dressed well and making your best appearance
- Identify your questions and answers for this interview

- Determine who you want to interview you as well as make a list of potential places you will seek to interview you

- Determine how to do a Video Interview

- Determine where to post your Video Interview

- Post the link to your Video Interview(s) within your Media Room

____
____
____
____
____

- Create a News Release for your Video Interview(s)

____
____
____
____
____
____
____
____

SP = Speaking

Each of the speaking venues will have their own checklist of items to do before, during, and after. And many of these have been covered in some of the code components within the formula. In order to modify whatever checklist you may want to use, you can refer to the various types of checklists and considerations that are developed as examples under the code components as examples of what you may want to include.

The following provides items related to high-level considerations for you to consider for a speaking engagement in front of a designation audience. If it is your own event, such as at a MeetUp or in a similar venue that you are putting on versus being a guest at someone else's event, your checklist will vary accordingly. It is important to identify speaking opportunities related to where you can leverage and grow your authority and your business leads, profits, and income.

Date of Speaking Engagement____

____

Organization____

____

____

Identify speaking topics related to your expertise_____________________________________

____

____

____

Type of Audience____

____

Core Message based on my speaking topics that address needs of the Audience

____

____

____

____

____

____

____

Checklist of items to do before the Speaking Engagement

- Follow up with the organizers
- Determine what items need to be onsite at the event
- Determine what to wear to the event
- Analyze the audience as well as what core message to provide
- Consider getting the Speaking Engagement videotaped and photo coverage

Checklist of items to do at the Speaking Engagement

- Arrive early

- Meet the organizers
- Test the sound on your mic
- Get a feel for the environment
- Be at your best during the Speaking Engagement

Checklist of items to do after the Speaking Engagement

- Send thank-you notes to key people related to organizing the event
- Get videotape segments edited to use for marketing purposes
- Post a brief video to your Media Room
- Get videotape transcribed in order to have the content to leverage.

Create a running list of places to speak at in the future, include potential places that may be repeats

____

____

____

____

____

Create a running log of places where you have already spoken

____

____

____

____

____

IMR = Install Media Room

Consider having your Media Room display your Media where what you want prominently displayed is recent Media as well as the highlights of your Media. Then, the others may be arranged first by Media type—such as by interviews, by articles, by books, by News releases, etc.—in a chronological manner. By keeping "Add Link to Media Room" in your checklists for each code component, you can more easily keep your Media Room updated so you know it is continually working for you to reinforce your authority.

It is also a good idea to keep a running log of your activities in a hard copy format as well as a digital backup any of audio, video and documents in case something happens with the website so you can reconstruct it.

Install a Media Room page to your website____

____

Add any prior Media you want to display____

____

Ongoingly post additional Links to your website

____

____

____

Keep a running log of Media Activities
[Note: Keep in mind that some Links may have a lag time before they become available. So make a note on your running log of which ones to follow up on so you get a Link posted once it becomes available.]

____

____

____

____

____

____

____

Save Media-related Audio, Video and Documents to your computer as well as have a backup

____

____
____
____
____
____

Consider what other type of Media to pursue that would be great to be able to display in the Media Room. Then, determine which code component type it best fits under as you refer to that section for tips of what items to consider in approaching it.

Authority Positioning

As mentioned elsewhere, once you have gone through the Startup Phase of creating your authority position, you will want to repeat these steps on a monthly and/or quarterly basis so that you continue to reinforce your authority, grow your business, and make a difference with your products and/or services. The following section on the Condensed Version of The Authority Code Formula can guide you to what are the essential codes to be able to repeat on a monthly basis during the ongoing Maintenance Phase.

With this type of compounding Authority Positioning, you become the undisputed authority on your topic because it is all there demonstrating your expertise, which is even stronger than being just a reference or a recommendation from a friend. You actually have established the foundation within The Media to back it up.

Maintaining Your Authority Positioning using The Condensed Authority Formula

In Chapters 12 and 13, the Condensed Formula is covered as an important part of maintaining, reinforcing and expanding your authority. This section of the application chapter is a reminder to refer to this formula while keeping in mind the importance of the overall formula as those code components will also need repetition. For easy reference, the Condensed Formula is included here as well.

The Authority Code Formula [Condensed for Monthly Repetition]

AA + IR + BSC + PR + OC+SP =
Authority Positioning Maintained

Refer back to Chapters 12 and 13 in addition to the application actions above as you plan for how to best apply and customize the steps in maintaining your authority.

The Authority Code Formula is proven to work—and it can work for you. However, there are a lot of details to manage for each of the code components, not to mention the learning curve for each one. To claim your authority more quickly and directly in a streamlined manner where you consistently build upon your authority platform can be achieved more successfully when you work with an expert with a proven track-record. If you work with an authority-building expert, it reduces the learning curve and maximizes the benefit you receive. By investing in yourself and your business, it should ideally pay off with more leads, more sales, and more profit if you position yourself well and take the right actions to make it happen.

You are already an authority—so claim it within your market using these power actions to increase your leads, your sales and your profits as you make even more difference!

Chapter 19 – Maximizing Leads, Sales and Profits

Various factors go into being well-positioned for managing the leads and converting them into sales. The main purpose of this chapter is to call your attention to how important it is to master this aspect of business as well as emphasizing the importance of becoming the authority as a key differentiating factor in overall success.

Being in a position to maximize on the leads you generate from your authority status is essential so you can impact the world with the value you provide as well as be able to create a successful business and lifestyle of your dreams.

There are additional books you can find that specialize in these areas. However, this book would not provide the full scope of what authority positioning entails if it did not mention the importance of being positioned and able to capture and track the leads generated from your authority status; having a sales system in place; and being able to increase your profit margin that provides you with business and lifestyle options.

Tracking Leads

When you claim your authority and market yourself as an expert, people in your target market want to connect with you—and many of them will want to do business with you.

Before they can do so, you need to have some key elements in place related to your business, including an online presence such as through social media and a website that has the capability to engage and educate viewers, allow viewers to connect with you, and enable them to buy your products and/or services from you.

Although the leads may come in from a variety of avenues—online social media, website, in-person networking, webinars, speaking, referrals from others, etc.—you can then track those leads and follow up with them in a systematic way that you develop around your business so you can serve them with consistency.

Making Sales

Knowing what you offer through your products and/or services is important so it is clear what you provide and people are able to know what they are to receive when they buy from you.

In order for them to receive some value upfront, you may offer something free with the incentive to buy another product and/or service from you at a great value.

It is essential to provide a marketing message along with your offer so they recognize the value and benefit they will receive.

By identifying the need in the market and filling that need with the unique way that you leverage your authority and expertise can help you make the sale.

As I mentioned, there are various factors that go into being well-positioned for managing the leads and converting them into sales. The main purpose of this chapter is to call your attention to how important it is to master this aspect of business as well.

What is often the case, though, is that people may be well-positioned for the sales, yet do not have enough leads because they do not market themselves effectively. The most effective marketing is to be the authority so that people hunt and seek you as the best—and are willing to pay more for your services.

Increasing Profits

When you receive increased pay for your services as well as more leads, you are in a position to have more profit—especially if you handle your income and expenses well.

Impacting The World

It—meaning your authority journey, your leads, your sales, your profits and your impact on the world—starts and begins with you because you are the one who can make the difference you can make based on how you recognize and utilize the power of your experiences and expertise as integral to your authority that allows you to make a difference in your market as well as in the world overall.

Chapter 20 - Introducing...You, The Authority

Although this chapter is the last one in this book, it is not "the end" of the book because it is actually the beginning of introducing "You as The Authority" as you continue to take the steps and invest in yourself and your business to make the most difference in the world with your unique gifts and mission.

This chapter is brief because it is your chapter to fill the blank slate of what is possible for you. As with most entrepreneurs, whether you are just starting out or are seeking to get to the next level, you may zig-zag some on your journey to what ultimate success looks like for you. Getting the right mentor support can help you take the right actions to shorten your learning curve so that your zig-zag begins to unite into the upward direction to create You as The Authority.

So that you have an ideal vision of what your desired success looks like, write a vivid description of what it looks like and feels like for you to be that authority as well as the lifestyle dreams that you have that accompany your vision.

With Me as The Authority, I...

____

____

Now, continue to implement The Authority Code Formula action steps to make your vision a reality!

Sometimes you may want to re-evaluate and adjust your ideal vision and corresponding plans because as you achieve new milestones you will have new vantage points along your authority journey that may enable you to see new opportunities further ahead.

It is worth emphasizing again that there has never been a better time in human history than right now to be an entrepreneur because you have the opportunity to broadcast to the world.

...And the opportunities are limitless when you apply The Authority Code to what you are passionate about as you build Your Legacy one Authority-Code Action Step at a time...

BONUS CHAPTER

Social Proof Viral Campaigns

For Authority Positioning

By Ken Rochon

Since the advent of social media, we technically live two lives. An offline life that we are used to and an online life that mimics the best version and perception of our offline life.

In this fast paced age of information, there is no shortage of content, just shortage of attention span. Marketers have the biggest challenges ever to distribute valuable content to the right audience and stand out enough to have them notice.

The only way to win in a game where everyone has content is to leverage the world to help you establish that your content is king. How does one accomplish this? I'm glad you asked. The concept is called 'Social Proof' and it is what it implies. It is proof in the social world that you are doing big things.

The big problem is as business professionals, leaders and influencers we have a habit of how we do things and if it works, why change it? The reason is that there is a lot of money being left on the table if you are not leveraging your offline moves to show up as social proof online moves.

A mindset that allows you to achieve this and create new online guerilla marketing habits is to think of your two lives you are living and are you feeding them and leveraging them so that there is congruency (integrity) between the two lives.

Take out your calendar of events and think about what you are doing offline and how it will show up online not just as content, but as social proof. And that it will go viral because it is leveraged correctly with influencers and leaders you are working with on the event and those that support you as strategic partners.

If you have friends in the photography and videography world, figure out how they receive value by helping you with your social proof. For instance, can you refer them to the event you are speaking or even attending? Imagine you got them a paying event, don't you think they would love to help show you are the star of the event?

Look at your social media, and if no one is talking about your page, chances are it is dead and no one even knows you are posting content (even if it is the best content in the world).

The magic of social media working is that there is harmony and consistency in the power and quality of your content and your distribution.

When content is level 10 and distribution is 0 or 1, you have what is called a 'Secret'.

When distribution is level 10 and your content is 0 or 1, then you have 'Noise'.

A secret or noise will not convert or make you proud. So make sure you have a great distribution strategist on your team so that you are leveraging your brilliant content.

If you are doing big things in the world, it is highly likely that you could enlist the help of college interns to follow you around and get key photos of you doing your thing. Interns are looking for experience and a means of demonstrating their competency with a portfolio. Your partnership with these interns gives them much needed experience and opens doors for them that otherwise would be challenging to open or even know about.

The game of social proof is likened to the game Malcolm Gladwell writes about in 'Outliers' and 'Tipping Point'. One is a calculation of 10,000 hours until you are the guru, the other is that there are so many actions that must take place for the results that were negligible become compounded to the point that you become top of mind, and get the best and most opportunities.

The third component or ingredient is the time relevancy of the content. If you are doing big things in the world at big events, chances are high that the ease of this content going viral correlates with the relevancy of the time to the event. The maximum viral happens because of the quickest, highest quality photo and content to appear with the most influence attached to the post. In other words, make sure when you post content, that you maximize all the factors, the quality of the content, photo, video, the speed of the content, and the leveraging aspects (including branding, commenting, sharing and tagging) the people in the photo.

About The Author

T. Allen Hanes

With roots from his Midwestern upbringing, T. Allen Hanes has traveled the world during his diverse and adventurous career.

Early on, he started out with several entrepreneurial ventures, although he soon thereafter aimed his drive and commitment towards serving for 18 years as a Media and Mass Communication Specialist, which involved being a top-rated Navy Photographer and Video Producer.

After he became a Retired United States Veteran, he founded and operated a highly successful Corporate Safety Training Program.

Currently, Hanes is the President of T. Allen Hanes & Associates, And The Authority Syndicate Group, LLC. Which enables him to be a Speaker and a Media Strategist while leveraging his International Speaker and Best-selling Author status as a #1 International Best-selling Author in both Marketing and Safety niches.

He is also a Director of Public Speakers Association.

Hanes enjoys teaching The Authority Code with its corresponding mindset to entrepreneurs across the globe to lead the way in showing them how they can awaken boldly and claim their authority.

He has a passion for helping entrepreneurs, business owners, authors, speakers, and coaches position themselves as the go-to person in their niche.

Since he and his team have helped hundreds of experts become Best-selling Authors, it is no wonder that Tracy is often referred to as "Mr. Incredible."

Hanes has been featured on *Forbes*, CNN, CBS, NBC, FOX and ABC as well as in *The Miami Herald* and *Small Business Trend Setters*, among other media affiliates.

He met his wife Linda in The Philippines when he was in The Navy. They have two grown children Trevor and Tiffany and currently live in Texas.

Hanes' hobbies include golf, lacrosse, automobile racing and football in addition to his passion for photography, video, and books—especially being able to use the book format to support others in sharing their stories and authority.

T. Allen Hanes, CEO
Positioning Expert & Media Leverage Professional
The Authority Syndicate Group, LLC. Recognition Strategists
Houston, Texas
www.ClaimYourAuthorityNow.com
www.meettallenhanes.info

Additional Information

For additional information about what T. Allen Hanes can do for you in applying The Authority Code so you more rapidly and confidently create your authority, please contact him at the following website:

www.ClaimYourAuthorityNow.com
To get started building your authority!

You can also find out more information about T. Allen Hanes as well as receive the FREE GIFT he has available on LinkedIn regarding specific authority-building Tips he shares directly with his clientele. Visit T. Allen Hanes at LinkedIn via the following:

www.TAllenHanes.com

On LinkedIn, you will also get access to a Special Offer on *The Authority Code Academy*, which is his massive online training course that goes into even more in-depth about how to leverage your authority. Simply connect on LinkedIn with T. Allen Hanes to get access to 50% off of the regular price of $197/mo. When you connect, he will provide you with a code that serves as the discount coupon. You then go directly to the course provided at the following website:

http://the-authority-code-academy.teachable.com

For other valuable information from T. Allen Hanes, visit the following websites:

www.TheIncomparableAuthority.com
www.iamtallenhanes.com
www.TheAuthoritySyndicate.com
www.meettallenhanes.com

T. Allen Hanes has helped hundreds of people leverage their authority and is confident that the information in this book and these sites can help you achieve authority status, too!

For additional videos and training go to
www.theincomparableauthority.com
To get started building your authority NOW!
www.claimyourauthoritynow.com

Photos

My Family During Recent Years

[L-R, My Son, Trevor (Audi Car Sales); My Wife, Linda (City of Galveston); and My Daughter, Tiffany (College Student in Texas)

My Family, Christmas 2015, Houston, Texas.

My Family During our Navy Days
Great Lakes, Illinois. 1994
Division Commander

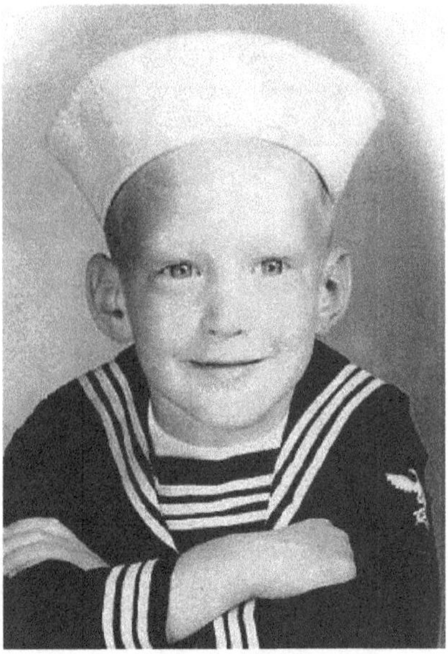

Was it destiny?
4 years old.

Active Duty Division Commander, Great Lakes, Illinois. 1994. 33 years old.

My Mother Sandra Kay with our Red 1965 Mustang, 5 years old, 1966

[Unfortunately, it was totaled when my Mother and I were hit by a drunk driver after this photo was taken]

My Father Charles "Russ" Hanes. Indianapolis, Indiana

The River Raft

My First Business Deal, Marketing Made Bliss. WNAP Raft Race, Indianapolis, Indiana 1974, I was 13 years old. $50 Sponsorship

Naval Class Photo in Pensacola Florida, 1989, (4th from right)

Motion Picture Cameraman Video Producer School

On the Aircraft Carrier
USS Carl Vinson CVN-70
1994 Western Pacific 6 Month Deployment

The Straits of Hormuz
Entering The Persian Gulf 1994

On the Firing Range in the Philippines, 1986

Retirement from US Navy
Great Lakes, Illinois Dec 31st, 1998

My first celebrity photo. Peter Lupus of the TV show Mission Impossible. 1972. I was 11 years old.

Speaker at Harvard Faculty Club, Cambridge MA. Business Expert Forum, Dec. 5th 2015

The Most Interesting Man in The World Jonathon Goldsmith. Harvard Faculty Club, Cambridge, MA. Dec 5th 2015

Dr. Joe Vitale, Multi Book Best Selling Author and star of the movie The Secret, Houston, 2015. Book Signing.

James Malinchak, Big Money Speaker and Dr. Bill Dorfman, Dentist to The Stars Las Vegas Event, 2010

Forbes Riley, HSN Host and Inventor of the Spin Gym, Las Vegas event 2010

Glenn Morshower, Actor and Movie Star of the Transformers, and 24 and many others.

Awarded National Collaborator of The Year for 2016, Public Speakers Association, June 2016. Palm Springs, California

As you move through your continued Authority Journey from leveraging your story and background experience to catapult your authority and success ongoingly, it is essential that you document that journal along the way so you make the most of your successes. If you do not have as many photos as you would like, just start now and build as you go.

Award-winning Authority figures make the moments memorable.

So, get started now applying The Authority Code and building your portfolio of photos and success...